A Cross by the Road

A Cross by the Road

Memoir of a Death Foretold

Jane Quint

iUniverse, Inc.
New York Bloomington

A Cross by the Road
Memoir of a Death Foretold

iUniverse books may be ordered through booksellers or by contacting:

iUniverse
1663 Liberty Drive
Bloomington, IN 47403
www.iuniverse.com
1-800-Authors (1-800-288-4677)

ISBN: 978-1-4401-9448-1 (sc)
ISBN: 978-1-4401-9450-4 (dj)
ISBN: 978-1-4401-9449-8 (ebook)

Printed in the United States of America

iUniverse rev. date: 1/11/2010

Dedication

Our son was born on June 23, 1959. We named him Michael James: Michael after his father, and James because it sounded like my name, Jane. Because father and son had the same first name, when our son was a small child we called my husband Mike and our son Mikey. For a while, father and son became "Big Mike" and "Little Mike." When our son grew up to be a muscular young man—bigger than his father—that distinction no longer applied. We didn't think "Old Mike" and "Young Mike" was nice. Our son wasn't a junior, so we couldn't call him Mike Jr. We also couldn't use "Michael," because he had a cousin named Michael. Although we often called him Mike, as most people did, sometimes for clarity, and always out of affection, those in the family also called him "Mikey." Our son died a tragic death on June 15, 1993, that devastated our family. This story is dedicated to Mikey.

Mikey at age 33

"... he who remains passive when overwhelmed with grief loses his best chance of recovering elasticity of mind."

Charles Darwin
The Expression of the Emotions in Man and Animals

Contents

Preface

Ten months prior to the accidental death of my adult son, I had a terrifying dream that foretold his death. I continued to have subtle premonitions that I didn't fully understand until it was too late. When my son died as the dream predicted, the entire family was devastated, and I was tormented with guilt because I had been unable to save his life. After fifteen years of unrelenting grief, I began writing this book as a form of self-therapy. The initial focus of my writing was on understanding the source and meaning of premonitions. I read hundreds of books about grief and death. I took a college course, attended self-help groups, and participated in conferences. I found scant information about premonitions of death, and often found an aversion to the subject. I finally decided to write the book I had hoped to find. Usually late at night, as I listened to the owls calling through the woods surrounding our home, I would sink deep into my memories. I found myself reliving all the joyful days of my son's life. My mind, which I believed had been shattered irretrievably, began to mend. Although writing this story helped me to understand premonitions, more importantly it helped me to heal by leading me to a new perspective about life and death. I hope it might also be healing to others who grieve an inconsolable loss.

Although I have changed the names of some persons in my story, the events depicted are true to the best of my memory.

Acknowledgments

My extended family has always been supportive through these many years, never making me feel I needed to "get over it." They, too, loved Mikey, and were stunned by his sudden death. Thanks to my sister, Sarah, who lit candles for him all over the world and who also helped me edit my manuscript. Many thanks to my nephew, Mikey's cousin Michael, who wrote a magnificent letter to us after Mikey's death, describing an experience they shared. My deepest thanks to my dear daughter, Peggie, for her insightful critiques and sibling perspective. Most of all, thanks to my loving husband Mike, who supported me as I wrote this book, as he has all my life.

Prologue

Beginnings are difficult to pinpoint. Perhaps this is because no event has a true beginning point. There is always a chain of precipitating circumstances that casts a shadow over the future. Where does the story of an individual life begin? At birth, at conception, when one's parents meet and fall in love? Or perhaps later, when one overcomes personal obstacles or finds his or her calling in life. Endings are also difficult to pinpoint. Those who have suffered the tragic loss of a loved one know the story does not end at death, but continues in the painful, insistent search for meaning. Beginnings and endings are those significant events that forever change one's perceptions and expectations about life itself. They are emotional explosions that alter the landscape and change the direction and course of life forever. This story begins with such an event, a premonition of death.

CHAPTER 1

The Dream

That is when it usually happens. You are in a profoundly deep sleep and something keeps nagging at you to get up. Maybe it is your customary wake-up time, and the habit prods at you. Yet there is a hazy awareness that it is the weekend, and you planned to sleep in after an exhausting week. So you ignore it. Maybe you have a vague feeling that it is really late and you should get up before the day is gone. Yet your mind gropes for any urgent plans and remembers none. So you try to ignore it. Then you dimly realize it is your nagging bladder, and it will not be ignored. The pressure is persistent and worsens until it forces you to attend to matters. That is how it was on that fateful morning in August of 1992. I managed to roust myself out of bed. Afterward, still bone-tired and groggy, I returned and sank down on the edge of the bed. The room was semi-dark because of the drawn drapes and cool from the humming air conditioner. It was quiet; no one else was home. Nothing needed my attention. I could not resist the still-warm sheets and slid back under the covers to continue my sleep. I drifted back across the threshold of consciousness into the hypnagogic sleep state where profound insights and prophetic visions often occur.

It seemed like minutes later when I bolted awake, shaking from a nightmare. My heart was pounding, my throat constricted with fear. I leapt out of bed and ran to the hallway in a panic. I tried to speak, but the words only came out in a choked whisper. "No, no, no, no, no, no!" There was no one to run to for comfort, no one to tell of my horrific vision. I stumbled back to the bed and clung to the edge of the mattress in stunned disbelief. Still trembling, I tried desperately to persuade myself that it was just a nightmare, but deep down I knew that wasn't true. It was not an ordinary nightmare. It wasn't even a common dream. It was a premonitory dream that portended my son's death, exposing my deep-seated fear of losing him. To quell my feelings of hopelessness, I resolved that I must take action. I had to warn him of the impending danger. I grabbed on to the knowledge that we were taking a trip that weekend to his home. Yes, I would tell him then about the dream. I lay back on the bed, closing my eyes to recall the dream and decipher its meaning.

For as long as I live, I will never forget this dream, but capturing the essence of it in words is difficult. Words are linear, following rules of grammar in an orderly, logical sequence. Dreams are synchronistic, flowing not by logic or laws, but by a hidden meaning that is coded in symbolism. Yet through the exercise of putting a dream into words, the mind must choose certain elements, and in choosing those elements the meaning is revealed.

The Dream

> The dream began with my husband, myself, and our son, Mikey, setting out for a boat ride on one of the many lakes near his home. We had recently given him the old Renken speedboat that we used on our many family vacations to Burntside Lake in Minnesota when our children were young. Mikey came to love being in the outdoors because of all the years we spent in those beautiful northern woods. In the dream, my husband was initially steering the boat, but the scene soon shifted. The dream pulled both my husband and me into seats toward the back of the boat as our son took over the helm. He was standing at the wheel, the wind blowing through his hair. I looked down, noticing how the edge of the boat cut through the gray water and churned up a spray of droplets. Ahead on the right there was an extensive bed

of reeds, with a waterway like a road through it. There were more beds of reeds farther off in the distance. I began to feel apprehensive, because we were going very fast and I could not clearly see what was ahead. Mikey was happy and unafraid. He always liked the thrill of living on the edge.

The dream shifted again. My husband and I were now pulled out of the boat into the upper balcony at the back of a dark movie theater. Our heads were silhouetted like cartoon characters against the large, brightly illuminated movie screen. When the movie began, the screen darkened around the edges, obscuring the background. I sensed my son's presence as he came into the scene; I somehow felt that he was still standing and moving fast through the air as if he were still in the boat. Everything was shrouded in black except for the sun shining like a spotlight on his face. He was looking back at us and smiling. A feeling of bliss washed over me as I realized how completely happy he was. As I lovingly watched him, I felt a strange sensation. I felt like I was inside his body and could feel what he was physically feeling. I felt the wind stirring his hair and streaming over his face and body as he cut through the air. I felt the tension tighten in his hands as his rate of speed accelerated. I felt as if we were one.

Suddenly, my attention was drawn far ahead to a field of tall corn in the distance to the right. The tops of the corn were being bent aside as if a hidden vehicle was coming through them at an angle. I became alarmed. I looked up and saw a huge rectangular transparent object flying fast and low through the air just above the field. I could not perceive what it was, but I could see the blue sky and clouds through it. As it came closer, I realized it was a monolith of unyielding, deadly force. I was immobilized by terror as I watched it speed toward my son. They were on a collision course, and he did not see it.

In horror I watched a huge radiator break through the corn at the edge of the field. The "camera" zoomed in on a dry, umber-colored substance that was being churned up alongside something gray. As I tried to comprehend what it was, a newspaper telescoped out of the sky, spinning in the way old movies dramatized a shocking event. It abruptly stopped, and the headline filled the screen: Fatal.

I lay there gasping at the horror. The overall message of the dream was clear. Our son had an accident, and it was fatal! The details were unclear. Did it happen on the water in the boat? Or by a cornfield when the corn was high? What was that transparent object? The movie scene had few helpful clues, but still I knew that somehow I had to warn him.

CHAPTER 2

Angola

Mikey lived in Angola, Indiana, which lies in the northeastern corner of the state near the Indiana Toll Road. The main tourist attraction in the area was the Pokagon State Park, a popular year-round resort. The park bordered Lake James on the west and south and Lake Snow on the north. These lakes linked into a chain of smaller lakes. Boating and fishing were popular activities. The beautiful beaches were ideal for swimming and volleyball. There was a formal inn, rustic cabins, RV hook-ups, and youth camping sites. There were also trails for hiking, bicycling, and horseback riding. The winter season offered cross-country skiing and a refrigerated twin toboggan slide. On the east side of the park was the Potawatomi Nature Preserve and Nature Center. Mikey took my mother and me there one year to see the live hummingbird display. He often gave his guests tours though the park, describing fascinating facts and places of interest.

Our family bakery business was in the northwestern corner of Indiana, near Chicago. It was a three-hour drive across the entire span of Indiana to get to Angola, but it was a trip we made countless times since Mikey moved there eight years earlier. His move to Angola had not been his first career move. Immediately after earning his electrical engineering degree from Purdue University in December

1981, he turned up in Texas. I don't remember if he told me about his plans or how he got there. There must have been a buzz at school about unlimited employment opportunities in Texas. In the late 1970s, Houston was the epicenter of the Sun Belt population boom. The 1973 oil crisis had caused an enormous demand for workers in Texas. Newscasts in the northern Rust Belt reported that so many job seekers descended upon Houston that tent cities had sprung up on the outskirts of the town as well as in the city parks and under highway overpasses. Before long, he landed a job at an electronics company in Houston.

Our daughter, Peggie, was in her final semester at Purdue. During spring break in March, she and I took a flight to Houston to visit Mikey. He couldn't wait to take us to Gilley's Club, a popular honky-tonk nightspot founded by country music star Mickey Gilley. Gilley's was made famous in the film *Urban Cowboy* that starred a new, young actor named John Travolta. While at Gilley's we rode the mechanical bull, El Toro, danced the two-step to a country music band, and soaked up the cowboy atmosphere. Mikey won a Lone Star beer at the "Hi-Striker," a device where you swing a sledgehammer to drive a weight high enough to ring a bell. He impressed a crowd of onlookers with the impact force he registered at the punching bag. He taught us the correct way to eat jalapeño peppers. The next day he drove us to Galveston on the Gulf Coast where I was amazed to see houses on stilts. Mikey related to us the history of the deadly Galveston Hurricane of 1900 that had killed thousands of people and reshaped the coastline forever. He loved history and was already immersing himself in the history of Texas. He soon had a beautiful girlfriend. Although I never met her and now don't remember her name, I have a picture of them posing together outside that most famous of Texas landmarks, The Alamo. Texas evoked images of legendary frontier heroes, sprawling cattle ranches, and wealthy oil tycoons. Everything about Texas was bigger than life. It was the kind of place that matched Mikey's expansive and adventuresome spirit.

Since Mikey had completed his studies midyear, in May he decided to return to the Purdue West Lafayette campus to participate in the formal graduation ceremony. Peggie would also graduate that May, having earned a degree in psychology. So brother and sister had the unique experience of taking part in the regal commencement fanfare together. I took pictures of them parading in the traditional walk across campus with their respective school cohorts. The sun was shining and the outdoor carillonic bells were playing school songs as they circled around the Loeb Memorial Fountain on the Purdue Mall. Mikey later told us that his supervisor was not pleased that he had requested time off to attend the graduation ceremony, but it was an important milestone to him. I am grateful now to have those pictures of that special day, the two of them together, smiling and optimistic about the future. On the wall next to my desk I keep a small golden framed photograph of Mikey in his black cap and gown, the orange engineering tassel hanging significantly on the right. I find consolation in remembering the joy of that sunny day so long ago.

Mikey, the Purdue graduate

Mikey's sudden return from Texas within six months was totally unexpected. In retrospect, I suppose it shouldn't have been, since his return had been foretold in a most unusual way. I had been invited by my theatrical sister, Sarah, to attend a birthday party for a photographer friend of hers. The party was held in his Chicago art studio where he lived and worked. The studio was decorated like a cluttered attic. Partitions of gauzy material were draped over sagging clotheslines, creating a maze of rooms. As entertainment, the host had hired a fortune-teller to do readings for his guests. The psychic's name was Marie. She looked like a gypsy with her wild black hair, long colorful skirts, and gaudy jewelry. Her glasses had coke-bottle lenses that magnified and distorted her eyes, making her gaze unsettling. Her purse was clipped to a long brassy chain that was double-wrapped around her body. I wondered whether she was forgetful or untrusting. I can't remember if she used tarot cards or a crystal ball, but I do remember one perplexing thing she said. She predicted that a fair person was coming back. I asked what she meant by "fair." She said someone with blond hair or blue eyes. Mikey had blue eyes, but I had no reason to think he was returning home, so I dismissed it.

A few weeks later Mikey was back home in Indiana. My first experience with a psychic had left me a baffled believer. Mikey never said why he was terminated. I was secretly glad he was closer to home, although I was sad that his first job ended badly. I later wondered if he was caught with marijuana or if he had been going out to bars and drinking and not getting enough sleep. Excessive alcohol use was a bad habit he picked up during his college years. He was always one to burn the candle at both ends. He was driven to live life to the fullest, to experience all that he could. He never appeared to worry about his grades or his job. I remember once complaining to him as I was on my way to take a test at work that the weather was so beautiful I'd rather be outside than inside taking a test. I was speechless when he said, "Blow it off, Mom!" That option never occurred to me. So, I suspected he may not have been worried enough about his first job performance review either. He still had the party mindset of a college student.

Houston, Texas, April 29, 1982

Peggie,

Well, I guess you've heard about my new car! It's a NEW '82 Camaro Z-28 with a V-8, 305 cu. in. engine with cross-fire injection, electric windows, electric mirrors, electric door locks, tilt steering wheel, T-top, AC, and *nice* wheels. The backseat folds down to provide more room under the hatchback. The color is dark blue with silver stripes along the bottom. Oh, well ... it gets me around.

Two weeks ago I got a speeding ticket for doing seventy-five in a fifty-five. But, that's nothing. Last Sunday I got two speeding tickets! The first was at 1:50 AM for going ninety-five in a fifty-five zone! Later on that day, about 8 PM, I was stopped for going seventy-two in a fifty-five mph zone. Fear not, because they were all in different counties (different judges). I hope I don't get my license suspended.

The bars down here always have good bands. For instance—Uriah Heep on April 16. Humble Pie at Rockabilly's last night, Joan Jett & the Blackhearts April 19, plus the usual good bands at Cardi's and Struts.

I am progressing rapidly in my job. As of now, there are nine people in the calibration lab, and there is a lot of competition for a single job. The scuttlebutt is that the engineer in mechanical R&D is going to get canned and that I am a possibility as a replacement.

I plan to come home for your graduation. I am going to ask my supervisor for Friday and Monday off so I can drive home. I figure it should take about twenty hours. We can party down when I get there! I hope everything is going good at Purdue with all your classes. I remember December '81 when I had so much to do before "the end." I look forward to seeing you on the 15th. Until then,

Hang loose,

Mike

Picture Mikey took of himself speeding in his Z-28 Camaro

On the other hand, many people were losing their jobs at that time. The population boom ended abruptly in Houston shortly after Mikey arrived there. The economy was beginning to sour from the oil glut, and the northern transplants were beginning to return home. As the Texas economy began to weaken in the 1980s, the rest of the country was sinking into a recession as well. The job market was also tight at home. The steel industry dominated the economy in our area and had been losing market share to foreign competition in recent years. Mikey went back to working at our family bakery while continuing to look for an engineering job. He would occasionally get calls from headhunters, but nothing materialized. One day in the bakery I noticed he was trying to hide the fact that he was distraught. I learned later that his Texas girlfriend had broken it off with him. She couldn't wait any longer for him to return or send for her. It was the first time I ever saw him fighting back tears. He was normally a cheerful, upbeat, quit-your-whining kind of person.

After nearly two years of searching, he finally found a position as a manufacturing engineer in Angola, Indiana. I remember his beaming face when I told him how proud I was of him. He said they were impressed with his work ethic when he told them he had worked in the bakery throughout high school and college.

Because the job was in Angola, he made a joke that he only got the job because he claimed he was fluent in Swahili. As we all stood there together laughing and hugging, inexplicably, I felt a shudder of apprehension go through my body. Startled by the incongruous emotion, I quickly suppressed it. I wanted to relish the joy of the moment. I was relieved and happy that he had found employment that used his education, even though once again it would take him some distance from home.

On a snowy day in January 1985, Mikey packed up a U-Haul truck to make his journey to Angola, Indiana. He loaded up all his belongings, his bedroom furniture, desk, wall map, pictures, bike and skis. I gave him an old Lazy-Boy chair, an end table with a lamp, and the black captain's chair with the Purdue emblem. His prize possession was his record player and a large collection of albums. Led Zeppelin, Rolling Stones, AC/DC, Black Sabbath, and Blue Oyster Cult are a few that I recall. He also had an extensive collection of history books about WWII and the American Civil War. Chess was his signature game, but he also relished war games like Axis and Allies, Risk, and Stratego. Some war games he created himself based on historical records of famous battles. He once cajoled me into playing a war game with him when his buddies couldn't come over to the house. He cringed at my mind-boggling stupidity at battle strategy. "Don't do that!" he would say hysterically. "You'll kill a thousand men!" Sometime during the loading of the U-Haul, our German shepherd, Spike, jumped into the rental truck and resolutely planted himself there. He was determined to go along, and it took much coaxing and finally a piece of liver sausage to get him back out.

Mikey and his dog Spike in U-Haul

Even after the packing and loading was complete, Mikey stuck around, wandering through the house, lingering. He seemed to be imprinting on his memory the scene he was leaving behind. I noticed the skies were turning dark and there was a deeper chill in the air as the wind kicked up. I feared that a snowstorm could soon make the drive treacherous. Peggie was going with him to help him move in, and I was anxious for them to get on the road. Bad weather didn't seem to scare him as it did me. One winter he had driven Interstate 80 across the Great Plains through a monstrous, life-threatening blizzard as the highway patrol was shutting the road down behind him. The road remained closed for days afterward. I suspected he was influenced to make that daring ride by the REO Speedwagon song "Ridin' the Storm Out."

I think he hesitated because he knew he was leaving home permanently. No matter how excited he was to follow a new path, he lingered at the point of departure. He hung back the same way on his first day of kindergarten. An older neighborhood kid had teased him as he approached school age, telling him he had to know all his arithmetic or they wouldn't let him in school. Too naïve to know the kid was joking, Mikey set about learning his numbers. He spent hours every day on the task, teaching himself to add, multiply, subtract, and divide—in that order. It was an unbelievable accomplishment for a four-year-old child. Still, on the appointed day, although certainly prepared, he clung onto me because he did not want to leave home. He lingered again when it was time to start his first semester at the University of Nevada in Reno. He knew right out of high school that he wanted to be an electrical engineer. I had advised him that Purdue University in our own home state of Indiana was one of the best engineering schools in the country, but he wanted to go out west. I thought back to the time when I had begged my father to let me go to the University of Chicago. I remembered how unrecognized I felt when he just dismissed the idea without a word of explanation, so I listened to Mikey and agreed he could go to Reno.

University of Nevada at Reno, October, 1, 1978

Dear Mom & Dad,

Well, here I am in Reno, Nevada! The town is very active and there is a constant flow of tourists through the city. They call it the "biggest little city in the world." Most of the town is made up of casinos, which are huge. You wouldn't believe the size of some of them. But, they aren't the only attractions one can see.

Lake Tahoe is so beautiful you have to see it to behold its splendor. I've been up there three times since I've been here. The lake is cold but clean. The reason why it's cold is because there is a huge ice pack at the bottom about three thousand feet down. There are beaches which dot the lake. You can't even see the south shore, but you can see the snow-covered mountains. I also went to Battle Mountain which is a city about four-and-a-half hours east of Reno. I went there with Geri, a girl I met at a fraternity party. We got to be pretty good friends, but don't worry, it's nothing serious. There are many more girls I haven't time to mention, but they are all around. I've made friends with a guy from Iran who is studying civil engineering and has been in America for ten months. We are pretty close and have a lot of interests in common, like girls and beer.

The college is small but very clean and modern. The academic standards are high. I got an A on my first physics test! Overall I've been doing very well in school. Well, that's all for now. I am glad to be out here. It's a good experience and a good college. Thank you for letting me come.

Love,

Mike

University of Nevada at Reno, November 13, 1978

Dear Peg,

I got your letter about a week ago, but I have been procrastinating. I've been having so much fun out here. I make a lot of visits to the casinos. All of the grocery stores and restaurants and bars have slot machines. There's even a place in town that has one-cent slots. So far, I'm about even on winnings and losses (which is good). I drink nothing but Coors beer. My partying with weed has calmed down considerably. I usually get stoned about once a week. There was a time when I didn't smoke any pot for three weeks! But, my cooler is constantly filled with beer. Last Saturday I went to see a concert with Pat Travis and Rush. It was fantastic. I hope the pictures turn out.

In school I'm doing well. I should have a 3.56 GPA for this semester. I really get into school, but sometimes (a lot of the time) I start to think of Indiana and Mom and I start feeling bad. I want to go to Purdue next semester. I've thought about it a lot and I feel that it will be best that I be home, close to Mom and Dad, and where I can relate to activities that are going on in Munster. The land out here is beautiful, but it's just not the same as being close to home where I can feel at home. Well, while I'm out here I might as well enjoy my "vacation."

> I enjoyed hearing from you. It's hard to think that my little sister is on her own. I hope you are enjoying Indiana State University and are having as much fun as I am!
>
> Love,
>
> Mike

On that snowy day in January 1985, he lingered once again, even though the U-Haul was packed and the weather was turning bad. He lingered in spite of the fact that he was glad to be resuming his engineering career. He lingered because he knew he would not be coming home again. One of his nicknames was "Last Minute Mike" because he always waited until the last minute to leave. He didn't like sudden breaks or traumatic transitions. Knowing this about his nature made the way he died even more heartbreaking.

CHAPTER 3

Lucky Man

Saturday, August 15, 1992, was the first weekend following my premonition nightmare, and I was still shaken to the core by it. Since we had previously planned to visit our son that weekend, I drove home from Illinois to meet my husband after he was finished with work at our family bakery. I don't actually remember making that drive because I was obsessed with my grim duty to deliver a life-and-death warning to Mikey. Apparently, at some point we got on the expressway that linked to the Indiana Toll Road and headed on our way to Angola. Although we were driving at maximum speed, the ride felt tortuously slow to me. The deathly premonition lay on my heart with the crushing weight of an ocean. It wasn't a message I could deliver by phone. I didn't fully understand the dream so I wanted to discuss it with him face-to-face—quietly—in private. Perhaps between us we could decode it. My husband was driving as he always did. Since we were typically quiet when we rode together, I don't think he noticed how deeply agitated I was. I knew I had to tell him about the premonition, but I had difficulty forcing myself to put it into words. He adored his son. It would be a horrific message to hear. Around the halfway point, as we came up over a hill and passed an RV campground near a small lake, I dredged up enough courage to speak. I hung my head so I didn't have to witness his reaction. It was so painful that I used as few words as necessary. "I had a dream about Mikey," I said. "He had an accident." I could feel my husband shake off his reverie and tense up. I steeled my resolve and whispered the worst part, "It was fatal." I could feel the atmosphere shift as it does when a cloud suddenly covers the sun. He shrank down into himself. His distress was palpable, but he didn't say anything. He did not laugh it off as nonsense or try to comfort me. He was stunned into silence. Since I didn't describe the dream itself, I wonder if my words had simply exposed his own unspoken fears of losing Mikey. After a few moments, I sat up straight and said, "I have to warn him!" I felt a tremor of resistance from my husband. He probably was afraid I would upset Mikey unnecessarily. Maybe the dream wasn't true! I could feel him having that same common sense argument I had with myself that it was "just a dream." But he did not try to talk me out of the dream or out of warning Mikey. Nor did he agree to help me deliver the message. He was shaken. We rode in silence for the remainder of the trip. In the days to come when we would drive past that landmark where I first spoke of my dream, I would inwardly recoil. It was as if that spot was charged with emotional residue like a battlefield at ground zero.

Mikey at Arapahoe Basin, Colorado

As we rode along, I searched for reasons to convince myself that Mikey could handle any life-threatening situation. After all, he had driven through that Great Plains blizzard unscathed. He moved to Angola during another bad snowstorm and had arrived safely. Peggie told me afterward that she was scared. "It was a nightmare! The roads were ice-coated, and there were white-outs! But I knew Mikey could get us through." Mikey loved to ski and chose the most daring slopes. I had a picture of him in the Colorado Mountains posing next to a warning sign: "DANGER! Hidden and Unmarked Objects: Ski with caution!" And, yes, he had survived a bad auto accident. Peggie and I always thought that the Emerson, Lake & Palmer song, "Lucky Man," was about him. Of course, I only knew one line of the lyrics, "Oooh, what a lucky man he was." I clung to the idea that he was a "lucky man." These thoughts took my mind back to that bad auto accident he had about four years earlier. I recalled that I had a strange experience at that time, as well. It was a dream, a fleeting image of my son lying face down in the mud. It was dark in the dream and there were emergency vehicles around with their red lights flashing. There was some type of pole, like a telephone pole lying on the wet ground next to him. The dream disturbed me because I couldn't tell if he was alive or not. I went into work the next morning in a troubled state of mind. I went to the office of a good friend and sat down to talk to her. She was the kind of person that I could easily talk to about any subject. When she noticed I seemed upset, I told her I didn't feel good. Both of my wrists ached, especially my right wrist, for no apparent reason. My jaw also ached. I felt out of sorts and anxious. However, she was preoccupied with a presentation she had to give at an early morning meeting, so we didn't talk about it further. My strange aches and pains began to ease.

A couple of days later I got a call from Mikey's girlfriend, Cristal. He was in the hospital in Michigan. He had had an accident in his little red Chevy pickup truck. He had been racing to visit her after work; it was dark, and the highway was slick from rain. As he was coming around a curve he slid off the road and hit a tree. His truck was totaled. He had hit and shattered the windshield. His right wrist and jaw were broken. Could I have had "sympathy pain" for something I didn't know had occurred?

After making sure Mikey was not in critical condition, I made plans to drive to Michigan after work and after the Chicago rush-hour traffic had died down. It was Thursday night, June 23, 1988, Mikey's 29th birthday. I made the five-hour drive alone. Neither my daughter nor my husband was able to come with me because of their work. Since it was a weekend in June, there were a hundred graduation and wedding cake orders at our bakery. My husband had to stay behind to handle the overwhelming amount of business and number of deliveries on his own. There was one very special wedding cake for our niece, Lizzie, who was getting married that Saturday. My husband had one living brother, Frank. Lizzie was Frank's daughter. Lizzie's mother, Dolores, had planned a garden wedding at their country home in Crown Point. It included a white horse-drawn carriage for the bride and groom. Mikey and his girlfriend had planned to attend the wedding, and we were going to celebrate Mikey's birthday afterward. Only my husband was able to attend.

It was midnight when I arrived alone at the hospital. A nurse directed me to Mikey's hospital room where he was asleep. His head was bandaged and his right hand was in a cast that went up to his elbow. I gently stroked his forehead. I didn't want to wake him. I was so relieved to be there and see that he was alive. As I was tiptoeing out of the room, he stirred and called out "Mom." I went back to the bed and assured him I was there. He pleaded with me not to tell Dad about the accident. He knew his dad's anger about his excessive drinking. His dad had berated him many times from about getting drunk. I then realized he must have been drinking at the time of this accident and that he didn't want us to know. I didn't know how long he had been in the hospital. When I went back out into the lobby I noticed a slender young woman in blue jeans sitting on a couch in the waiting room. I had never met Mikey's girlfriend before that day. Cristal was a natural-blond beauty who wore no makeup. She spoke only briefly to me. "Mike didn't want me to call you." I was thankful that she finally decided to call us anyway. At least that time, I was there for him. I wanted to know more about what had happened, but Cristal looked tired and left for home. I stayed over the weekend with him in his hospital room. Cristal dropped in during visiting hours. We knew there was an important wedding we were missing. Cristal grouched that she had bought a new dress for the occasion.

"I never wear dresses. Now I'm stuck with one I will never use!" I thought her focus was odd under the circumstances. I chalked it up to her disappointment at not meeting Mikey's family as she had hoped. You can imagine how pleasantly surprised Mikey and I were when Lizzie and her new husband stopped in the hospital to visit the day after their wedding. I was very touched by their compassion for him and for us. How many newlyweds would have taken the time on the first day of their honeymoon for such a visit? It spoke to what they valued most in life. I have never forgotten their kindness.

Mikey back at work with broken wrist and wired jaw

When Mikey left the hospital his jaw was wired shut and his right wrist was in a cast. He subsisted on a liquid diet and learned to write with his left hand. Over time I learned that this was not the first time he had been arrested for driving under the influence, but it was his first DUI accident. In June, 1985, just five months after starting his new job in Angola, he was arrested for operating a vehicle while intoxicated. His driver's license was suspended in Indiana for thirty days, and he was required to undergo alcohol counseling. In July, 1986, he was arrested again for operating a vehicle while intoxicated.

His driver's license was suspended in Indiana for six months. Now this accident was his third drunk driving incident. He was not allowed to drive in Michigan for five years. He was further ordered by the court to undergo alcohol rehabilitation or go to jail. He gratefully chose treatment for alcohol addiction. Since he could no longer drive into Michigan where his girlfriend lived, Cristal moved in with him in Angola. She did not smoke or drink. She provided important moral support to him as he struggled to overcome alcoholism.

CHAPTER 4

Alcoholics Anonymous

Although I was aware over the years that Mikey drank too much, I didn't realize how extreme it had gotten because he lived so far away from home. He got started with alcohol and drugs in high school, at a time when teenagers tend to experiment with forbidden things and when drugs were just beginning to be a problem in the high schools. His drinking was kept largely under control because he was on the varsity swim team. The Munster High School swim team was the Indiana State Champions for all four years Mikey was on the team, and Coach Jepson had strict rules against alcohol and drugs. Mikey's alcohol use escalated dramatically when he went away to college, partially because he had no parental supervision and also because of the rampant drinking culture on college campuses. Over time, he became severely addicted.

Since I had no personal experience with alcohol and certainly not with drugs, I was oblivious to the symptoms of alcoholism. I grew up in a home where there was no alcohol. The one exception was a bottle of "firewater" my father kept hidden high up in a kitchen cabinet. He took it down each Christmas and took one swig as we watched in wide-eyed amazement. I didn't know how to deal with Mikey's drinking problem. I usually approached it with logic and reasoning. I told him, "It's not good for your health," "You might kill yourself or someone else," and "It's a waste of money." I thought drinking was something he could control if he just realized the consequences. When reasoning didn't make an impact, I once asked him why he drank.

"It's a reward!" he proclaimed. I sort of understood what he meant. I regarded chocolate as a reward, even though logically I knew the consequence of eating too much was added pounds.

My husband's situation was the opposite of mine. His father had turned to alcohol when the family was displaced after World War II. When my husband was about eight years old, the family was uprooted from their home in Romania and forced to migrate by covered wagon across Europe to the safe American zone in Austria. It was a journey that took seven weeks. Along the way their caravan was shot at by Serbian Partisans and bombed by English fighter planes. Although they left behind all their possessions and their friends, they escaped with their lives. Like most displaced persons during wartime, they were very poor. There were no jobs, no food, and no hope. When his father got drunk, he was very abusive. His mother committed suicide after the accidental death of her seventeen-year-old son made her harsh life even more unbearable. Because of his childhood experience with alcoholism, my husband had little tolerance for drunks. His way to deal with our son's drinking was to get very angry and call him names. The humiliation only made Mikey's drinking worse.

Mikey began his court-ordered treatment for alcohol addiction at a dependency treatment center in Fort Wayne, Indiana. It was an in-hospital rehabilitation program espousing the philosophy that alcoholism is a disease. The treatment process aimed to increase awareness and motivate change. He stayed there for twenty-eight days. Afterward, he was introduced to the twelve step program of Alcoholics Anonymous.

> November 1, 1988; Alcoholics Anonymous—Step One: We admitted we were powerless over alcohol—that our lives had become unmanageable.
>
> I acknowledge that I am powerless over alcohol. It has become clear that I cannot control my drinking because when

I drink, I like to drive reckless and fast. This has caused me to be arrested three times for DUI and caused me to nearly kill myself and others. I have gotten into several fights in the distant past because alcohol gave me the false feeling of power and boldness. The only times that I have argued with my wonderful girlfriend was when I was drunk or when I was drying out. Drying out made me feel like I was giving up something special and I had to blame something for forcing me to give it up, like my girlfriend or the law. I have missed work because of drinking and staying out all night. My company will not send me to Japan on business again because of it. The strong desire to drink has not left my mind, but it has eased somewhat as this is day thirty of being dry.

I do not like when I cannot remember what I did. I do not like to lose control of my mind. It seems especially hard for me because I remember only the good times. Drink controls me by turning my thoughts to the good times. One example is the time I quit drinking for fifty days. I was tempted to drink by Tim who had left Angola a few months earlier for employment in Chicago. He came back to visit me and some other friends. He suggested drinking and playing golf. I did not want to seem like a party pooper and *quickly* agreed. We started drinking "rattlesnakes" and then drove to the golf course. I was in my red S-10 and he in his white S-10. We got lost and ended up racing all over Steuben County until we found the golf course where we drank beers. Then when we were leaving, Tim said, "Last one home is a rotten egg." I was alone in my truck and I raced like a bat out of hell for home. Some asshole was going twenty mph on US 20 and I passed two cars on the berm and flipped him off. A cop pulled me over, and that was my second DUI. It cost me five weekends in jail, lawyer bills, a fine, court costs, alcohol counseling, one year suspension, and higher insurance costs.

I could go on about the time I totaled my red S-10 and nearly killed myself and two old ladies and spent six days in the hospital, or the time I got into a fight in Hessville and somebody got shot, or the time in Calumet City when I beat the shit out of a guy and his friends had to kick me off of him or I would have killed him, or the time I smashed my Z-28 into a parked car and sped away because I was drunk, or the time I had a blackout and made an ass of myself by sneaking into the girls' dorm at Purdue then misplaced my van, or the

> time Gerald and I were banned from Skip's bar for thirty days, plus dozens of other experiences. I just leave it to suffice that I know now that I cannot control my drinking and that I have reasons to quit. Let me not forget that if I am found drunk the court will lock me up for at least one hundred eighty days!

The Alcoholics Anonymous program emphasized that the solution to a drinking problem is not found through individual will power, but through a higher power. Step two of the program states, "Came to believe that a power greater than ourselves could restore us to sanity." However, this higher power was defined by the individual. Some could call it God, others could think it is the AA group itself. I was surprised how deeply this idea affected Mikey. He was never religious; our family was never religious. I did not believe in sending small children to Sunday school because I saw it as nothing more than indoctrination before a child was capable of thinking for himself. Religious beliefs taught at such a young age are so deeply ingrained in the psyche, that one never is free from them. My mother felt it was important to send us to Sunday school, and like all children I listened to Bible stories, went through catechism, and at age twelve became a member of the church without true comprehension. As I grew up I felt angry that my young pliable mind was filled with irrational ideas before I could examine if they were true. And when I did examine them, I couldn't force myself to believe. As hard as I tried to rid myself of my religious indoctrination, fragments of it were still floating around in my brain, impeding my search for meaningful spirituality. I wanted to teach my children to use their intelligence and compassion to find a genuine spiritual philosophy. So I purposely did not send them to Sunday school. I thought they would let me know if and when they wanted to learn about their religious tradition.

However, when the kids were young, we lived in the same apartment building as a very religious family. Their Baptist faith encouraged proselytizing. They talked to Mikey about going to their church when he was about nine years old. Their church was huge, a forerunner of the massive mega churches of today. It took up a square city block in the downtown section of Hammond, Indiana. It had a large fleet of buses that picked up the children in the greater area on Sunday. Actually, I had gone to vacation Bible school as a child at that same church one summer. I remember feeling lost in the massive auditorium full of strangers, but I did love the songs we all sang together. I still remember the lyrics about the wise man who built his house upon a rock, and the itsy bitsy spider that went up the water spout. So, my feelings of the church were not all negative, and I allowed Mikey to go. At first, Mikey was happy to attend. He thought he was learning some wonderful truth, like when he learned about numbers. However, within a couple of weeks I could see that he was disillusioned. I asked him what was wrong, and he said all they cared about was how many more kids he could get to come with him. Every time he got on the church bus, the driver wanted to know why he hadn't found more kids to bring along. To avoid that interrogation he stopped going. The church lost an opportunity to teach a spiritual lesson to a child who was eager to learn. Knowing his initial disappointment with religion, I was surprised that he responded so fully to step two of the AA program.

> Angola, Indiana, November 13, 1988
>
> Dear Mom,
>
> I took three weeks off of work to enroll in an alcohol and substance abuse treatment program in Fort Wayne. I am writing to you from there and by the time you get this letter I will have been discharged.
>
> I am an alcoholic. My drinking and drug use has caused a lot of changes in my personality and my life. The accident I had in Michigan happened because I was drunk and driving too fast. I was not drunk enough because I remember some of it and flashbacks of it still haunt me. I am grateful that I did not harm anyone else or kill myself.
>
> Alcoholism is a disease, not a lack of will power. My previous attempts at sobriety, on my own, over the past two years have failed. Once I quit for seven weeks and the day I started to drink again, I got a DUI. I have come to realize, through this program, that because of alcohol my life has become unmanageable. Part of the program involves believing in a higher power. You know how bellicose I get when it comes to God and religion. But, I decided to give Him a chance. He proved He exists, to me, through an experience that I will

relate to you later. The God I discovered is personal to me and I do not plan to become a religious fanatic or try to force Him onto you or anyone else.

I have gone six weeks without alcohol or drugs, so far, but it will be a long road to recovery and I must take it one day at a time. I plan to go to AA meetings (Alcoholics Anonymous) three times a week to help me recover and they do help a lot.

Please do not be offended if I do not want to drink alcohol when I come over and don't try to force it on me because I'm still weak and I may succumb very easily. I have not had this problem with you, but I have with my father. I am writing a similar letter to him so you will not need to force the issue with him.

I look forward to my new life without alcohol or drugs. It will be difficult for the first year or two but I plan to start saving money and doing more things with my girlfriend. I did not tell you that I was entering this program because I needed to be alone with my thoughts and because, as always, I do not want to make you worry.

There are a lot of things in life that I feel I missed and I am fortunate that I recognized my problem as a young man. Over the past six years my thoughts have been clouded by alcohol and drugs. I have a lot of talents and have gone far on them. Just think how much farther I can go without alcohol and drugs! If any of this is troubling you, please don't hesitate to call me. I have always loved you and I am thankful that you put up with my problem all these years.

Love,

Mike

That November Mikey drove home to spend Thanksgiving Day with us. This was a Thanksgiving we had much to be thankful for, and I planned to give thanks in style. Mikey brought his girlfriend, Cristal. It was the first time she joined a formal family gathering. Grandma loved to talk and commented that Cristal was too quiet. She barely spoke a word the entire visit, but I was always the quiet one when growing up, so it didn't bother me. What I noticed was that she kept her arms folded across her body all the time. It was a defensive stance. Her body language implied she wasn't comfortable or open with us, but I was sure we could get her to warm up to us in time. I also noticed that she stood slightly hunched as if she thought she was too tall. It's true she was tall, but she was slender and pretty. Mikey seemed to like tall, willowy girls. Both he and Peggie were a little on the short side of average height. My sisters always told me I had the most beautiful children. They were both blessed with striking good looks. Mikey had dark hair like mine and "laughing" blue eyes like his father. He had a strong athletic build from his years of swimming. Peggie was a blue-eyed blond with a perfectly proportioned figure. She was fortunate to get her father's thick, naturally-wavy hair that she wore in a Farah Fawcett style. Peggie brought a dinner guest who was rather homely and shorter than any of us. He played a guitar and idolized Willie Nelson. I laughed when Peggie joked that she had only one rule for a guy she would date: "He has to have a waist bigger than mine!" My sister Carole and her young daughter also joined us. I asked her not to bring her customary wine. I wanted to make sure there would be no alcohol around. Turkey dinner was Mikey's favorite, and I prepared all the traditional trimmings. I set an elaborate table with our best china, candles, and the gold-rimmed crystal water glasses he gave me for Christmas one year. I remember he had on a white dress shirt with blue pinstripes. When it came time to mash the potatoes and carve the turkey, Mikey rolled up his shirt sleeves and pitched right in. I wanted to find something for Cristal to do so she could relax and feel like she belonged. "Can you make the white sauce for the Brussels sprouts?" I asked her.

"That's one thing I know how to make," she answered sardonically, belittling her own cooking skills. Peggie candied the sweet potatoes and made a cherry topping for her famous cheesecake. Everyone scurried around and got all the food on the table. I said a special grace that included remembering the first Thanksgiving and the Indians who made it possible. Thanksgiving had a little extra meaning to our family because I was a Mayflower descendant. Being a history buff, Mikey took pride in that information until he learned that there were millions of Mayflower descendants in the United States. Finally, we all dug into the feast.

Mikey piled his plate a couple of layers high and ate with relish. "I haven't had a decent meal in ages!" he announced. Cristal looked a little embarrassed, but no one really felt his point was to fault her. He just loved turkey.

After dinner a few of us sat around the table to talk. I still remember sitting next to Mike and noticing what broad shoulders he had. As promised, he told me of his spiritual experience of a higher power. He told me that he prayed with all his heart to God to take the desire to drink from him. He said it felt like a heavy weight was lifted off of his shoulders, and he was relieved of his desire to drink. He said before he prayed he had desired a cigarette, but that desire was also gone. He thought a moment then added, "I think time stood still while I prayed to Him and the miracle was done, because I looked at my watch before and after my prayer and noticed that no time had elapsed. I was awestruck at the incredible supernatural power, and I was convinced that there is a power greater than myself that can remove the desire for alcohol. That night I quietly thanked Him for helping me. I feel a love for my higher power and a security that it is there for me, when I need it." As he spoke I could tell how deeply he was affected by this spiritual experience.

This epiphany was a turning point for Mikey. He quit alcohol, smoking, and drugs all at the same time and never took them up again. Everyone supported him. His family, his friends, and his coworkers repeatedly congratulated him and sent cards with penciled in notes:

"Happy over one hundred days!"

"One year!"

"We knew you'd do it, but want to be sure you know we're proud of you!"

"You're in our prayers!"

"You did it! I'm very proud of you!" As each year passed he celebrated the milestone with a candle in a Hostess Twinkie. Although we are certainly lucky that Mike was not killed in that bad accident in 1988, the accident turned out to be a blessing. It led to his participation in Alcoholics Anonymous, which changed his life. He didn't talk much about it, but he made sure that he surrounded himself with people who supported him and avoided any environment that was a temptation. I quietly marveled at the maturity and serenity I felt in him. He knew he would succeed, and succeed he did. He remained clean and sober the rest of his days.

January 3, 1989

Dear Mike,

I wanted to thank you for the lovely gifts and to say how much we loved having you and Cristal home for Christmas and Thanksgiving. Thank you so much for driving that long distance to be with us. Holidays just aren't holidays without family. I've had much to be thankful for this past year, but of all those things, your giving up alcohol is the best gift of all. Your courage and perseverance are an inspiration to us all. I keep you in my prayers always.

I hope to have a fiftieth birthday party this summer—black balloons and all! I hope you will be able to come.

Love to you both,

Mom

CHAPTER 5

The Warning

We finally arrived at Mikey's home in Angola around noon on August 15, 1992. Although I could not get there fast enough, once I got there I didn't know how to deliver the message. The welcoming scene didn't match my desperate mood. Everyone was so happy to see us and there was such a flurry of activity. There didn't seem to be a right moment to bring up the subject of the dream. Mikey was a happily married man now. He had married Cristal the previous December. When Cristal told me she got tears in her eyes when he proposed, I started thinking of wedding plans. Music, merriment, and celebration! Peggie would surely be a bridesmaid, probably in a turquoise dress—Cristal's favorite color. Then one day Mikey informed us that they were married by the Justice of the Peace at the Angola court house just before Christmas. His best friend and coworker, Eric, and his wife Cara were the witnesses. Mikey sent me pictures of them in casual work clothes taking their wedding vows. They had a wedding dinner for all of us the following summer at the Das Dutchman Essenhaus in the heart of Amish country. Although I never asked, I always wondered why they married that way, since Mikey loved parties. I think it was his concern that there would be drinking at a big party, because Cristal's brothers-in-law were heavy drinkers. He was determined to keep alcohol out of his life.

Mikey had planned a cookout for our visit that day and had also invited Eric and Cara and their newly adopted baby girl. Mike had just bought a new ranch house and seemed to enjoy every aspect of being a homeowner. He was enthusiastic about his landscaping. He had planted the small pine trees Peggie had given him as a housewarming gift. He gave us a tour inside the house to see all the changes. He had already installed the blinds that were our housewarming present. The blinds were needed to block the intense heat that poured in through the sliding patio door in the dining room. He proudly showed us the beautiful wooden headboard he made for the waterbed. It was solid oak with sliding panels and a mirror in the center. He loved working with wood as my father had, and kept a well-organized workshop in the garage. There he had refinished an old rolltop desk my father had made out of scrap wood during the Great Depression. I used to play under it as a child, and when Mikey got the desk it was old, worn, and wobbly. The transformation to a thing of beauty was amazing. The desk was in use again in his home office along with his drafting table. The kitchen was large enough for a small dinette table in the corner. Although Cristal said she had become a pretty good cook with the aid of Hamburger Helper, carry-out menus were still hanging on the refrigerator near the phone. They had prepared the customary picnic fare: baked beans, potato chips, hot dogs, and cheeseburgers with all the trimmings. We sat outside on the deck drinking soft drinks and iced tea while Mikey did the grilling. I was still trying to find the right moment to talk to Mikey alone.

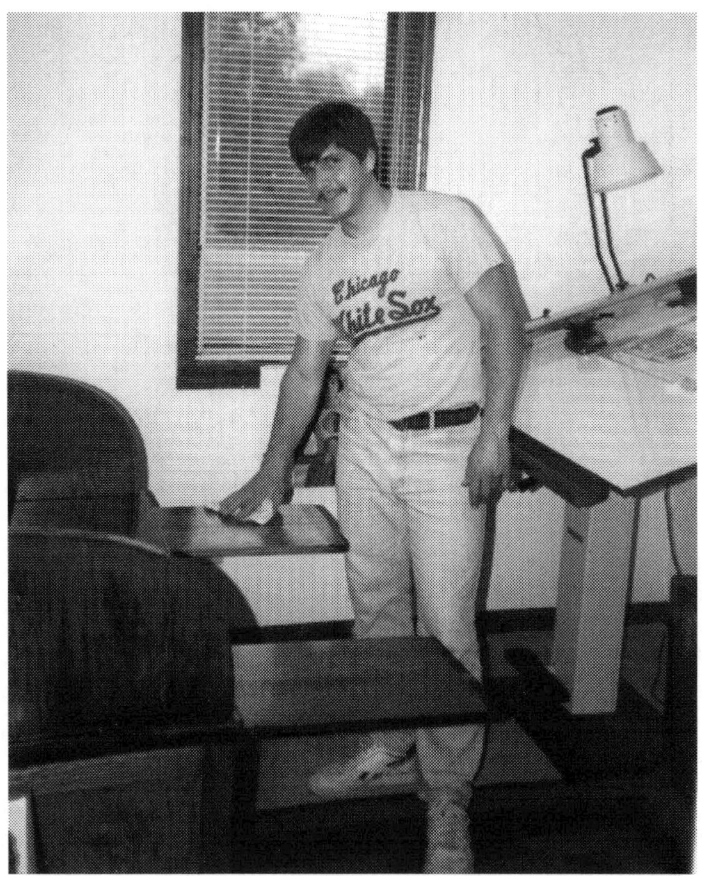

Mikey at the rolltop desk he refinished

As the afternoon wore on, it became increasingly hot and humid. The deck faced the south, and it had no canopy. We soon had to retreat back into the house to finish our meal in the air-conditioned dining room. At some point the baby needed her diaper changed. It was a dirty diaper. Eric was going to handle the challenge, and he called Mikey to come and learn the ropes. Mikey and Cristal wanted to start a family and had been trying to have a child. Mikey hung back nervously while Eric laid the baby on the kitchen table and prepared to demonstrate the procedure. Everyone was out in the kitchen laughing and joking and holding their noses, while I sat alone in the dining room, sullen and brooding. It had been days since I had that horrible premonition, and I could not shake the foreboding. It's hard to put that feeling into words. The closest expression I can find is "mortal fear." I associated the idea of "mortal fear" only with a battlefield until I experienced it myself one night. As I sat alone at my kitchen table one evening, with the back door slightly ajar to allow the spring breeze to flow through, I was suddenly overwhelmed with fear for no obvious reason. It was as if I sensed the presence of someone bent on murder lurking in my backyard, which bordered a public path. A terror of such magnitude gripped me that I couldn't see straight. I think adrenaline must affect one's vision, because I felt like my eyes were glazed over like those of a fox when cornered by the hounds, realizing it is about to be torn to shreds. I slammed the door shut and resisted the urge to hide in the closet. When the feeling of terror passed, I wondered if my imagination had gone berserk. I was vindicated when I learned the next day that my next-door neighbor had called the police that same night because she saw the handle on her kitchen door being turned. Since the moment I had bolted out of bed from the dream, I had been in the grip of something that was like mortal fear, except that which I feared seemed to be all in my mind.

The laughing and joking seemed to go on so long I could stand it no longer and burst into the kitchen. From across the room I blurted out to Mikey, "I had a dream that you had an accident!"

He stopped, rather startled at this off-the-wall remark, and then just laughed it off saying, "It was just a dream!" I was shaking. My husband was standing at the side of the room and looked very apprehensive, but he didn't say anything. Mikey told me many times I worried too much, and he reminded me again. "Mom, you worry too much!" It is true. I had worried about him all his life.

Almost from the day he was born I had worried that I would lose him. Perhaps it was the tenuous circumstances of his birth. Perhaps it was because he was my firstborn and my first experience of that deep love a mother feels for her child. I knew that losing him would kill me, and this realization made me feel vulnerable. Around those who envied me, I was temperate in my display of affection. I didn't want any enemy to know my Achilles heel. I did not want the gods to know I loved him more than I loved them, lest they take him from me in jealousy. The fear of losing him continued as an undercurrent throughout his life, and I whispered a prayer every day to God to protect him. I continued to pray every day until he was thirty years old, thinking that surely by then he would be safe.

Mikey was now thirty-three, yet I was beside myself with worry because of a dream. It possessed me. I could not set it aside. As I stood there in the kitchen feeling very alone, I became aware that everyone had stopped talking. No one knew how to react to my strange behavior. In the glare of normalcy I started feeling like a nut. Why was I acting so crazy over a dream? My behavior was unreasonable in the face of the facts. I didn't have any details, just a feeling. Mostly it was because Mikey wasn't alarmed that I began to doubt my certainty. He didn't take the dream seriously. He thought I was just worrying needlessly. I began to realize I was in some kind of altered state of consciousness, and I started to question my sanity.

This wasn't how I planned to deliver the message. My bizarre behavior caused disbelief. Their reactions confused me. My God, it was such an important message! Or, was it? What was the message? Why should I believe he would have an accident again? He had turned his life around since that bad accident in 1988. He had stopped drinking, stopped driving recklessly, continued to attend AA meetings, and briefly joined a church. That summer he had started a physical fitness program of diet and exercise. He liked shooting basketball after work, lifting weights, and riding his mountain bike. He was looking into teaching swimming lessons at the local community college. He proudly refused to take any more financial help from us, paid off his debts, and saved enough money to buy a house. He got married and planned to raise a family. He got a promotion at work. In his last performance review his boss had told him he was a "prize." He was happy, productive, and responsible. Having another accident didn't seem likely in his new straight-as-an-arrow lifestyle.

Maybe I was stressed out. I had taken a voluntary one-year leave from my job as part of a downsizing program at work. The telecommunications business was having rough times financially and began temporarily reducing the workforce in an effort to stay competitive and survive. It was the era of globalization. Our jobs were being shipped overseas to cheaper job markets in India and Poland. We were even required to train our replacements. Maybe I was more stressed about job insecurity than I realized, and it showed up in a dream about my worst fear. I retreated back into the living room with a sense of conflicted relief. I wanted to be wrong. I wanted to believe I was overreacting. No one wanted to hear what I had to say anyway. I pushed the dream down as far as I could. Down, down hard until it was suppressed. Yet, I still felt it lurking there, hidden deep in my soul.

I don't recall what we did the rest of the day. We must have decided to take a boat ride, because I remember feeling apprehensive about getting in the Renken speedboat. I remember Mikey encouraging me to get on board after my husband wanted me to stay on shore because I seemed to be in a bad mood. I didn't want anyone to go, but they were going. I finally came aboard because Mikey asked me to, and I wanted to be with him if something should happen. I was relieved to get back to shore after the boat ride. Mikey may have taken us on a drive through Pokagon State Park around the chain of lakes. I vaguely remember staring out the car window at the scenery, but I really didn't see what was before my eyes. How can you enjoy yourself knowing the world is going to end? My only comfort was being with Mikey, having him safely near me and seeing how happy he was.

Later, as we were preparing to leave, I went out and sat on the wooden steps that led from the house to the garage. I had failed in what I believed was my mission. I was confused and anxious, like someone having a mental breakdown. Mikey came out a few minutes later and sat down beside me on the step. I think he realized I wasn't happy and came to comfort me. He asked me about the courses I was taking. As part of the voluntary one-year-leave package, the company agreed to pay for any educational courses. I always loved college. I was known as a "professional student." I decided to study sociology, something completely different from my previous majors in mathematics and computer science. Mikey asked me if I planned to teach, and I said I thought I would. He was so gentle and encouraging with me, telling me to do what I loved to do, to follow my dreams. For a moment I felt like the parent-child role was reversed. The conversation was very comforting to me. "I think the accident was in the boat, but I am not sure," I said suddenly. I didn't even know I was going to say that. It just bubbled up from my troubled mind. I cringed, thinking he probably had enough of that silly talk. He wasn't offended, but he didn't respond. I worried I was scaring him. In frustration, I pushed that dream down again and decided to stop thinking about it. I was to find out in time that he never took the boat out again after that day. It sat covered with a tarp in his backyard and became a nest for raccoons.

CHAPTER 6

Daydreams

I lived in the older part of the town of Naperville where some of the houses are over one hundred years old, many in disrepair. The old neighborhood surrounds a quaint downtown area with sturdy stone shops lining the picturesque river walk. The economic and social focus of the town is a small private community college that bustles with activity during the school year. Everything is within walking distance, including a commuter train station just three short blocks from my house. I was finishing my master's degree in sociology at the University of Illinois and taking the train into Chicago to attend classes. I loved that walk along the uneven sidewalk in the crisp autumn air. I often stopped in the small old-fashioned corner store that sold homemade cookies and salads and the world's best bratwurst. All the trees in the neighborhood were massive, with branches that stretched from yard to yard and arched over the street. The leaves turned a brilliant gold in the fall. As you walked under their high canopy of branches, it felt like you were walking through a floodlight as bright as sunshine. Our front yard had one very large old maple tree that shed piles of leaves every year, leaves that had to be raked to the curb for pickup. I loved to rake leaves. Raking the brown dry leaves, smelling their earthy scent, and hearing their crunchy sound was meditative to me.

When I felt sad I went outside to rake leaves. I lived alone there in an old house. I had moved to Illinois in 1985 when I resumed my career, but I remained there while on leave and attended school. During the week my husband stayed in Indiana in an apartment behind the bakery. He was still operating the bakery but was planning to retire as soon as he found a buyer. We saw each other on weekends when we could. After my dream, I had fallen into a depression, a melancholia which turned my thoughts to the sad things in my life. Our marriage wasn't very happy at the time. I never really understood why and ceased trying to figure it out. We were slowly drifting our separate ways. As I raked and raked, the long metal tines scratching against the earth, I found myself making a bargain with God. I vowed that I would quit complaining about anything and everything. I would not complain that my husband didn't seem to love me anymore. I would not complain that I was not able to go to medical school. I would accept my lot in life and never complain again if only my children were kept safe. With tears in my eyes I pleaded to God to protect my children from harm. I know I said "children," but it was really Mikey I was most worried about. Although I did not think about the dream anymore or try to decipher its meaning, deep in my soul I was still deathly afraid.

My routine was to watch the five o'clock news on TV every evening. I would lie down on the couch in the dimly lit den with a blanket and pillow. Hanging from the sill outside the window was a flower box filled with wave petunias. It was near the end of the season, and the flowers were now fading and going to seed. Among the drying stems, a small hummingbird whirligig was still active. Its plastic wings formed the propellers that would rattle and spin earnestly in the intermittent breeze. Often I would daydream to that lonely haunting sound.

I would find myself reminiscing about Mikey when he was a child. Different images would spontaneously appear in my mind. He was a very fussy infant, maybe colicky, and the only way I could quiet him was to walk or rock him almost constantly. He was born in the summer, and I remember rocking him in Grandma's rocking chair and singing "Summertime" from the musical *Porgy and Bess*.

We were poor young parents, and I smiled, remembering the words. "Your daddy's rich and your momma's good lookin' ... so, hush little baby, hush now don't you cry."

I remember his first Christmas when he was just six months old. I cradled him in my arms and just marveled at him. I didn't think I could love anything so deeply. I remember the summer day I told him he was now three years old and showed him how to hold up three fingers to show his age. I remember tying his Buster Brown shoes as we got ready to go to the park that day. I pushed his baby sister Peggie in her stroller while he rode standing on the back. In pictures he always had an arm around his little sister or was holding her hand. He was protective of her and never showed sibling rivalry or jealousy toward her.

Mikey at age 3 holding Peggie's hand

The winter he was three and a half he began to count and make detailed charts of all the numbers. We had a meter stick that had inches up to thirty nine on the reverse side. He would get stuck at thirty nine. I remember so many mornings before dawn he would appear at my bedside in his blue flannel pajamas and ask me, "What comes after a three and a nine, Mommy?" Half asleep I would say a four and a zero. That happened so often I finally decided I had to explain how the numbers progressed. I was a math major, after all. He understood it until he got to ninety nine. So, another lesson was needed. After he got the system, he would count all the time, everywhere. He would be in the back seat of the car as I was driving on errands, counting and counting. Eventually, it started to drive me nuts, so I'd ask him to please stop for awhile. He would be silent, but occasionally I would hear some numbers slip out, "… 542 … 543 … 887 … 888 … 1,253." He counted and counted, and he drew meticulous charts with boxes for the numbers. He was obsessed with numbers.

Then one day he started teaching himself arithmetic. As I washed dishes in the kitchen, he would ask me to give him addition problems. So I would make them up, and he would answer enthusiastically. Then he moved to multiplication. He would announce his findings with a question. "Do you know what three fours is?"

"No, what?" I would ask. And he would proudly claim that it was twelve. Finally, I got smart and started asking him how he knew that. He would explain that if you have three cars in a row, and each car has four wheels, then you have twelve wheels. He announced one day that two fives is the same as five twos using his fingers to demonstrate that truth. The commutative law of multiplication! That was quite sophisticated thinking for a four-year-old.

When he moved on to subtraction, once again I gave him problems while I washed the dishes. One day, by accident, I gave him a problem that had a negative answer, "What's five take away seven?"

He got mad, and said, "Zero."

I smiled and said, "Well, then what is five take away ten?"

He got mad again and said, "Really zero!"

"How about five take away one hundred?"

Frustrated, he said, "Really, really, really zero," and stomped out of the room. I thought I would now have to teach him about negative numbers. We had a thermometer outside the kitchen window, so I stood him up on a kitchen chair to look at it. I showed him that there were numbers below zero and you said "minus" for them. When I set him back down on the floor, he had such an amazed look on his face as if I had told him such a remarkable thing. I reminded him of that many years later, and he said to me, "Well, yeah. I realized there were twice as many numbers!" I had to laugh. He continued to surprise me with the way he thought about things.

I never really could get him to tell me how he divided. He just did it. Once, I accidentally gave him a problem that did not divide evenly; of course, he got mad. So I told him if something was left over we would give it to our cat. He was pleased with that solution. I would ask him, "What is eleven divided by five?"

"Two with one for the cat," would be his answer. Eventually, he would get a little upset if there was nothing left for the poor cat.

His final announcement to me before he started kindergarten was about numbers that are "all together" and numbers that are "not all together." I asked him to explain what he meant by that. He replied, "Numbers that are 'all together' can be put in twos, and numbers that are 'not all together' always have one left over." I realized he meant even and odd numbers, so I taught him to say even and odd. He told me that when you add two even numbers you get an even number. If you add two odd numbers you get an even number. If you add an odd number and an even number you get an odd number.

I told one of my professors this once, and she said, "I have college kids who don't even know that!"

A skeptical coworker once asserted that he must have learned all his arithmetic on *Sesame Street*. I told her there was no *Sesame Street* on TV at that time, only *Bozo Circus*, which he would give up to discuss numbers with me. The truth is, he taught himself arithmetic while lying behind the living room couch using straws and a mountain of determination. Needless to say, when he started kindergarten he astounded the teacher. I used to wonder why I was so fortunate to have such a mathematically gifted child. I was a math major, but I never displayed such precociousness or even much of an interest in numbers as a child. I felt especially blessed to have a child who was so enthusiastic about learning.

As the days passed into winter, I found myself reminiscing about Mikey nearly every evening as I relaxed on the couch. I never grew tired of going over and over the same memories. I thought back to those heady days in high school when he was on the swim team. I spent four years attending swim meets. The winter swim meets were held indoors in hot, steaming pool rooms where I got so drenched in sweat I nearly froze when I went outdoors in the frigid air to go home. The summer swim meets were outside in the stifling heat, where I once got a severe sunburn. I didn't care. I wanted to soak up every minute of Mikey's sports events. The state swimming championship was held at Ball State University in Muncie, Indiana. I remembered the excitement I felt when I clicked my stopwatch and knew he had placed to swim the breaststroke in the finals. Munster High School won the state swimming championship all four years he was on the team. Each time we made an elaborate three-tier cake in advance that declared Munster the winner. I decorated the cake with red fondant seahorses, the team mascot, and put a large red number one on the top tier. The team came to regard this cake a good luck charm. In fact, the year following Mikey's graduation, the new team requested that the cake be made for them. Our bakery donated the cake, and Munster High School won that year, as well. That was the last year I made the cake, and the five-year winning streak finally came to an end.

Mikey winning the state swimming championship

I started to wonder why I was only reminiscing about Mikey and not about my daughter. I thought back to the cute things she did as a toddler. I remembered when she was two years old, and a rotten-toothed neighborhood bully ripped Mikey's sunglasses right off his face. Mikey collapsed in tears, but Peggie was not standing for such an atrocity. She told the bully off and retrieved the sunglasses. Such a little fighter for justice! I remembered once when she pointed at a bag of marshmallows and asked, "Can I have one?" I had told her what they were called the previous day and said she could have one if she could remember its name. She stared at it awhile and finally announced, "Marshpillow!" I was delighted with her creative answer and gave her two. The family has called them marshpillows ever since. Yet, as hard as I tried to redirect my attention, my mind soon drifted back to Mikey and the most beautiful memory of all. I remembered the sunny summer day he was born. I remembered how thrilled his dad was the first time he saw him in the hospital. He had wheeled me down to the nursery in a wheelchair where we looked at him through the glass partition. There were other fathers there, silently looking at their tiny, rosy babies wrapped in pink or blue blankets. My husband was not silent. He was literally dancing with joy up and down the corridor. "Look, he moved his hand!" he loudly boasted. He could not stop rejoicing over his newborn son.

In January of 1993, Mikey and my husband took their traditional yearly ski trip together. Mikey loved skiing. Ever since he was a teenager he had skied at places like Big Powderhorn in upper Michigan and Winter Park in Colorado. My husband, who grew up in Austria, was an avid skier. He gave Mikey lessons. That January they planned another trip to Winter Park. Since driving could be treacherous across the open plains in the winter, I suggested they try taking the train. They could pick up the California Zephyr right at the end of my street in Naperville and take it right into the ski resort at Winter Park. They agreed. They stayed at Beaver Village Lodge. I have an album full of pictures my husband took of Mikey on the slopes. "Get me with some air!" he told his dad. My husband lay down on the snow to get an outstanding shot that showed the shadow of Mikey's airborne skis against the snow. When they returned a week later, I picked them up from the train station just down at the end of my street. It was an easy way to travel, but Mikey complained that the train ride was too slow.

My husband told me later that as they were riding home, he was just watching his son as he looked out the window at the passing scenery. He was so happy to be spending time with him that he whispered a prayer, "Please, don't let this end." It was to be their last ski trip together.

Mikey at the Winter Park ski lodge

CHAPTER 7

Premonitions in Spring

Peggie decided she wanted to further her education by getting her MBA at the University of Illinois in Chicago. She was living with me in Naperville at the time and working at a flower shop close to home. She could have taken the commuter train into the city, but chose instead to drive. I truly admired her determination and her courage at driving into the city at night to attend classes. After earning her MBA, she landed a very good job in human resources at an electronics company in a nearby town. She decided to get her own place closer to her job. Batavia was an old river town built along the steep banks of the beautiful Fox River. We often took bike rides from our house to her apartment along the extensive bike path that followed the river for miles. She rented the downstairs of a house in the older section of town. We helped her move and decorate the apartment. She painted the kitchen an apple green, and I made some curtains for her in an English ivy pattern that matched her dishes. We painted the bedroom sunshine yellow like the bedroom she had as a teenager. We took her celery-green French provincial bedroom set out of storage and moved it into her new place. The set had a post bed with an ivory crocheted canopy, two dressers, and a desk with a hutch. Her bedspread was an ivory-colored polished cotton with a full skirt that draped on the floor; the matching curtains had abundant ruffles along all the edges. On the floor was the Axminster wool area rug that had survived water damage when a pipe broke at our home in Munster. It was a deep green with an ivory lattice pattern. It was a beautiful room and the most completely furnished room in the apartment. The dining room was separated from the living room with an archway flanked by white Grecian pillars. Peggie's nickname was Pegasus, and she had a Pegasus collection she displayed in the dining room. She was interested in photography and had several black and white Ansel Adams pictures hanging in the living room that were striking against the gray walls. She seemed pleased that she finally had a place all her own.

Early in the spring of 1993, Peggie called me on the phone late one night in a panic. She was hysterical with fear from a nightmare. She could hardly speak. She was living alone, so I couldn't ask anyone to comfort her in person. I tried to be as calm as I could and asked her to describe her dream. She just kept saying she didn't know, she didn't know. It was just so frightening. I asked if she could remember any details. She said she did not, but her bedroom had an acrid smell that terrified her. She said the smell permeated the air. It was the smell that had jarred her awake from the nightmare. That alarmed me, and I wondered if there was a fire smoldering in the apartment somewhere. I reasoned that the wiring could be bad in an old house. I asked her to go around to each room and see if something was burning, check the stove, check the electrical cords. She came back to the phone and said the smell was only in her bedroom. "Actually," she said, "it's hard to explain but it seems like it's just inside my nose." I didn't know what to think of that, so I asked her what it smelled like. She groped for words and finally said it was like burning rubber, like a burnout on the road. It was the smell that terrified her. I tried to calm her down, but she was inconsolable. She was crying and said, "I am not sure, but I think it had something to do with Mikey." I really don't know why I didn't make any connection to my premonition, but I did not. Perhaps it was because the speedboat and water were so clearly defined in my dream. Besides, I had firmly pushed my nightmare down months ago and felt more concerned now about a possible fire. I had never told her my dream, so she could not have made any connection either. We never talked about it after that day. It was just an odd thing that fell off the radar.

> Orlando, Florida
>
> April 15, 1993
>
> Dear Peggie,
>
> Cristal and I are in Vero Beach, Florida. The weather has been perfect for our first four days. We are going to Cape Canaveral today. Wish you could be here.
>
> Love,
>
> Mike and Cristal

When Mikey took a vacation to Florida in April with his wife, my husband offered to stay at his new home and watch it while they were gone. We had finally sold the bakery business so he had more free time to do whatever he pleased. My husband had always wanted to open his own bakery, and had worked at several of the bakeries in the area, adding to his repertoire of products. When a bakery came up for sale in a Polish neighborhood in East Chicago, Indiana, he was ready for the challenge. The immigrant clientele appreciated a baker trained in Europe, and his business was very successful. The first day we opened there was a line of people down the block waiting to enter the crowded store. There wasn't a crumb left at the end of the day. Our whole family was involved in the business at various times. I hired the salesclerks, kept the books, and paid the bills. I even learned to decorate cakes in a pinch when our decorator was hospitalized. Both our children worked in the bakery in the summers during high school and college years. Mikey learned the production end of the business working right alongside his dad, and also helped make deliveries to caterers. After I resumed my telecommunications career and moved to Illinois, Peggie scheduled the employees, decorated cakes, and did the payroll. Cousins also served a stint in the bakery. Cousin Karen became a talented cake decorator. The boys worked in production in the back. Uncle Mike wasn't easy on any of them. They scrubbed pans, mopped floors, kneaded loaves of bread, fried doughnuts, and manned the huge oven in a room with no air-conditioning. When bakery "boot camp" was over, they would boast that they survived a real job with a real boss. The bakery was mostly successful because the boss himself worked so hard. He was determined to do well and be a success. It was his American dream. Yet, because of the long night hours, he had missed out on many school events over the years. He missed all of Mikey's swim meets since they were on Saturdays, the busiest day in the bakery. After twenty years he decided to fully retire at the age of fifty-six and enjoy the things in life he had missed. While he was house-sitting at Mikey's house that spring, he noticed the new black Trek bicycle Mike has just purchased. It was in the basement, unused. He told me many years later that he got the strangest feeling as he looked at that bike and said under his breath to it, "Don't you hurt my son!" Although I had told him about my dream months earlier, he never mentioned his brief premonition to me at the time. He probably thought he was just being paranoid.

Last Mother's Day visit with Mikey

The family all met at Grandma's house for Mother's Day on May 9, 1993. Mikey and Cristal drove to Hammond from Angola. We arrived from Naperville. Mikey had been adhering to a health regimen and looked very fit. I fondly remember that he was thrilled to show me some engineering drawings he had made in a Computer Aided Design (CAD) class he had just completed. He enthusiastically rolled them all out on the living room floor and explained what they were. It was in the weeks following that Mother's Day gathering that I began hearing some strange sounds in my Naperville house. It always occurred on a weekday when my husband was not at home. During these weeks he was in Indiana assisting the new owner of the bakery. The first time it happened was in the evening when I sat down to watch the five-o'clock news. I heard a big bang, like something had fallen on the roof of my two-story house. I thought it might be a branch of the old maple tree, so I didn't think much of it. Branches were always falling off that tree, but usually only in a rainstorm. It had been sunny and calm all day. About a week later, I heard the same sound again at the same time of day. This time it was much louder, and it sounded closer, like it might be inside the house. Reluctant to get up, I stayed on the couch, trying to figure out what could make that sound. I thought maybe my huge medical encyclopedia or dictionary had fallen off the top shelf of the high bookcase in the next room. I thought it was peculiar that it should suddenly fall. I got up to look and discovered the book had not fallen. I could find nothing that could have made that noise. I didn't know what to think of it. Since my husband was not home, I could not ask him what he thought it was. The third time it happened was a week later. I heard the same sound at the same time of day. This time it was so loud that I jumped off the couch. The sound frightened me. This time I actually went outside the house to see if something had fallen off of an airplane and hit the roof. I walked around the house, looking on the ground and up at the roof. I found nothing. There were no neighbors looking out their windows as if they had heard something. Perplexed, I went back inside and upstairs to the second floor. I saw nothing amiss. I looked in the attic to see if something had come through the roof. There was nothing. This time I was shaken. I turned off the TV and analyzed that sound. The sound was the same every time, a sort of double beat, a softer first beat then a very loud second beat: da–DA, da–DA, da–DA. It always happened at the same time of day, when I lay down on the couch to watch the evening news. I could make no sense of it. It left me unsettled. When my husband came home that weekend, I told him about the incredibly loud sound. He also investigated and found nothing amiss. After the third time, I never heard those sounds again.

Mikey and his dad sifting soil for garden plot

At the beginning of June, Mikey called me to tell me he needed some more bricks to finish the walkway through his new garden. He had become very interested in organic gardening. During the time my husband was house-sitting he had helped Mikey sift all the heavy clay soil to remove the stones for a garden plot. Mikey had then engineered the garden with precision, drawing up a detailed chart that identified each plant and the date it was planted. He now needed sixteen more yellow bricks from the extras we had on hand and wanted to know if I could bring them to Angola. I asked him how soon he needed them. He said, "Pretty quick." I decided to come right away. It was a long ride for sixteen bricks, but I wanted to go see him and the weather was nice. I asked my mother to come along for the ride. She was in a wheelchair and rarely got out of the house, so she was happy to go. We often took rides in the country when we were growing up. It was a simple pleasure we both still enjoyed. We took the back roads that were less traveled but more scenic. We drove through Amish country, where we shared the road with so many black one-horse carriages I almost felt like I was in a time warp. The drive took longer than expected, so we arrived just as Mikey was coming home from work. That day Grandma gave Mikey a Civil War soldier's sewing kit that belonged to a relative who had fought in that war. She knew how much he liked history. Mikey wanted to show me some beautiful irises he had planted at the corner of the house. They were a gorgeous pale peach color that I had never seen before or since. Again, I felt such serenity in him. He was unusually quiet, and I sensed he felt deeply at peace with himself and his life.

After we ate dinner, Mikey showed me where he had set up his stereo system in the basement. He had me sit down in a chair strategically located to get the full benefit of the stereo sound and played "Eminence Front" by The Who. It was fantastic. I laughed when I remembered that was the same music playing the day he and Peggie almost burned down the house. That day I had gone out shopping, leaving my teenagers at home alone. Mikey had put a steak and hash browns on the stove to cook and then went upstairs to his bedroom, shut the door, and blasted "Eminence Front" full volume. Peggie had joined him in his room for the raucous session. When the music stopped, they looked at each other and both said, "What's that noise?" They opened the bedroom door to hear the smoke alarms screaming. The steak and hash browns were in flames on the stove and smoke was billowing through the house. As I pulled up in my car, I noticed the windows, both downstairs and upstairs, were open. Mikey and Peggie were desperately trying to fan the smoke out of the house before I returned home. I have always associated that song with Mike and those crazy teenage years.

When my mother and I returned from that trip to Angola, I decided to take my car in for some bodywork. The plastic shield under the front bumper had been damaged in a most peculiar way. Some hardened snow had flown off the roof of a van traveling some distance ahead of me on the expressway. The flat sheet of icy snow came sailing through the air and hit under my front bumper. I was surprised how hard it shook the car, because I expected just soft snow. I was also surprised at the damage it did. Six months had passed, and I had never bothered to get it repaired. That week I felt compelled to get it fixed and took it to a local body shop. They were a little backed up with work, so I didn't expect it back for a while. I decided to splurge and have them fully detail the car, as well. I felt a need to have my black Mercedes all polished and in perfect condition.

CHAPTER 8

The Sailboat Party

June 12, 1993

My husband bought a sailboat shortly before he sold the bakery and retired. It was a daring purchase, since he knew nothing about sailing at the time. It was a used twenty-nine foot S-2 that he found in dry dock at a boatyard in Chicago. He and a sailor friend brought her home through the locks of the Chicago River. The iron bridges spanning the river in downtown Chicago had to be opened for the tall masts of sailboats making their way out to Lake Michigan. My husband said there was only one gatekeeper who had to run from bridge to bridge to open the numerous gates along the way. It took nearly seven hours to traverse that short distance! When they finally emerged into Lake Michigan they were met with a bad storm. As the boat was battered by high waves, water started pouring into the cabin from the water tank hose that inadvertently was left open. My husband manually pumped the bilge, wondering what he had gotten himself into! Finally, they made it safely to their home port in East Chicago, Indiana.

We named her the "Edelweiss" in remembrance of Austria, the country he left behind when he immigrated to America. I was thrilled with the sailboat, and I drew an edelweiss flower for a decal at the bow. I never imagined we would be so lucky to own a sailboat. We docked the Edelweiss at a small marina near the bakery where we had a permanent slip. My husband always made friends easily, and he befriended a group of men who docked their sailboats at the same marina. He learned how to sail by sailing with them. He was the kind of person who learned by doing rather than from books. However, he also took the Power Squadron course to learn about the boating rules, courtesy, and safety. Every day that the weather was good my husband was out on the water. He had a natural talent for sailing and soon became an expert captain. He quickly picked up the sailing jargon just as he had easily learned five foreign languages as a child in Romania. I often told him, "You should have been a translator at the United Nations!" He loved languages and took pride in learning to speak proper English.

I also loved sailing and was willing to endure the long drive over the congested Chicago expressways to spend the weekend on the Edelweiss. Sailing was so calming to me. The gentle lapping sound of the water and the rhythmic rocking motion eased away all the tension that built up during the corporate workweek. After a peaceful day on the lake in the fresh air, I would crawl into the v-shaped bed under the bow and fall asleep, listening to the gentle clanking of the halyards on the mast. I felt like a child in a cradle.

Every September we participated in a sailboat race to Michigan City that was sponsored by the yacht club. There was one race that I will never forget. We experienced every type of weather over the two days. We had sailed to Michigan City in beautiful weather, making good time. The beach that evening was lit by a Hunter's Moon. As we slept overnight on the boat a cold front came through, bringing an autumn chill in the air. When we awoke in the morning, everything in the marina was coated with dew, including the hundreds of spider webs that hung like jeweled necklaces from the railings along the docks. The air was muggy as the return race began. We sat in a dead calm for two hours just outside the harbor, tormented by thousands of biting black flies. When the wind finally picked up it was so light that the sails kept luffing as we crawled along. When we were finally out in the open waters, a sudden storm with sheets of pelting rain came sweeping across Lake Michigan from the northwest, building up giant gray rolling waves. We had to get the sails down before the boat capsized! The jib was on a roller furling so my husband quickly rolled it in. The main sail had to be taken down manually. The boat was heeling heavily as my husband hung on the boom to pull the sail down. I clutched the slippery helm, trying to keep a 270 degree heading against the gale. In the back of my mind I was asking myself, "Now, what did he say to do if he fell overboard?" Fortunately he got all the sails down, but then the boat started turning leeward. He turned on the tiny three-horsepower motor, but it didn't have enough power to propel us forward in such rough waters. We were going nowhere and getting drenched by the cold rain. My husband decided we needed a little sail if we were ever to get home. He let out a tiny triangle of the jib to catch some wind, and we took off going at more than six knots across the lake. As we sailed back into our home port over an hour later, the rain subsided and the sun came out. I had never been through anything like that on the sailboat. We had been caught in the sudden fury of Lake Michigan, yet so much was happening that I didn't even have time to be afraid. I felt I earned the right to call myself a sailor that day.

Everyone we knew was invited to take a sailboat ride at one time or another. Sisters, nieces, nephews, friends, and coworkers all sailed with us. A few were terrified by the occasional "knock-down" and never came back. Some were impatient with the slow pace, but most enjoyed it. My sister Clarissa and I spent one Fourth of July anchored out on the lake after dark where we could watch the firework displays in all the communities along the southern shore. Peggie lived in Illinois and came when she could. Mikey lived even farther away, but made time to go sailing with his dad. Mikey quickly learned all the ropes. Being young and strong he could winch up the mainsail and unfurl the jib faster than I ever could. He could make a tack without getting hit by the traveler on the boom as I once had. He knew how to trim the sails so the tell-tails were just right. It pained my neck to look up so far, and I never had the patience for it anyway. When coming into dock, he could easily jump from the moving sailboat to the pier to tie the boat to the bollard. I was not agile enough for that. Mikey was a perfect first mate for his dad.

That spring, my sister Carole's daughter, Caroline, had just completed medical school at Rush Hospital in Chicago, and her immediate family members traveled from various places across the country for the graduation ceremony. Carole wanted to do something special to celebrate while everyone was in town. She called me and asked if they could go to the marina and have a sailboat party there. The weather was good, and Caroline liked to sail. In fact, she had once taken a week-long sailing trip up the eastern shore of Lake Michigan with my husband. It was a perfect setting for her party. It was a totally spontaneous gathering.

On Saturday, June 12, 1993, everyone headed to our sailboat at the marina. Carole was divorced from Caroline's father, who still lived in Florida. He drove to Indiana for the special occasion with his new wife and old dog. We had fond memories of him from when we all were newlyweds, and we were happy to see him again. Carole's son Michael drove in from Arizona just for the graduation. Michael was a unique, creative, and very intelligent individual. He had majored in geology and civil engineering in college and started a geodetic consulting business. He liked the wild, desolate places devoid of people. He and Mikey had hiked the Grand Canyon together one year. Carole had remarried and had another daughter, Cynthia, by her second marriage. Cynthia was ten years old at the time of the party.

Two of my sister Clarissa's adult children were there: Jimmy, who came with his wife and step-daughter; and Karen, accompanied by her husband Rick and their three-year-old daughter Karrie. My mother was there, sporting sunglasses and worrying about being on the wobbly pier in her wheelchair. My childhood girlfriend Judy was also there. We had known each other and been friends since we were three years old. She was like another sister and attended many of our family gatherings.

It was pure luck that Mikey and Cristal were there that day. I can't remember exactly why they were able to attend, but I believe they were heading home to Angola after a small vacation in Wisconsin. Since they would be passing by the marina, they planned to stop in briefly to see Dad. When Mikey heard there was going to be a party, he decided to stay and join in. It was pure luck that Peggie and I were there that day. I had not planned to drive to Indiana that weekend as my car was still in the repair shop. When the idea of the party at the sailboat spontaneously materialized and I knew Mikey would be there, I wanted to go. I needed a ride and asked Peggie if she would go with me. She was a little reluctant at first because she always liked a lot of advance notice about things. I remember telling her, "You'll be sorry if you don't go." I really don't know why I said that, or what

I meant by it. I probably just meant she would be missing a good time. As further persuasion I said I needed her to take pictures. She was the photographer of the family. We drove to the marina together in her black Chevy Camaro Berlinetta.

Throughout the afternoon, my husband took small groups of people out on short sailboat rides. He could only take as many people as there were life jackets on board. I made sure I went on one of those rides when Mikey was among the group. The waves were gentle, and we sailed eastward, hugging the shoreline. As the Indiana Dunes came into sight on the starboard side, I was watching Mikey and noticed how he seemed to be taking in the beauty of the landscape. I was momentarily reminded of the way he acted whenever it was time to leave home, as if he was taking in every detail and imprinting it on his mind. He seemed pensive, as if he was seeing it for the last time. I wondered about it but assured myself that he was probably just tired from his travels.

Mikey and his cousin Michael on the Edelweiss

Peggie had a high quality Canon EOS camera and took wonderful pictures of that day. As I look back at those pictures and see all the smiling faces, I could see that everyone was enjoying themselves. There were pictures of Mikey and Michael, the two cousins, standing on the deck of the sailboat as it was heading out of the harbor. There was a picture of Mikey and my husband gazing affectionately at each other. There were clusters of various partygoers toasting with cans of soda. As I look at those pictures now I feel a dissonance with how I actually experienced that day. As the day wore on, I felt a heavy mood descend upon the scene like a strange, invisible fog. Carole also noted that there was something peculiar about the air that day, something hanging over the party and the people there. It felt surreal and ominous.

It came time for Mikey and Cristal to start the long drive back home to Angola. I was standing next to Mikey on the pier, and we were looking out over the water. He turned toward me and said, "I've started riding the bike again." When he said those words, I started shaking like there was an earthquake inside me. To this day I cannot truly explain what happened to me at that moment. Try to imagine standing right next to a train track and being unafraid because there are no trains in sight. Unbeknownst to you, there is a huge invisible freight train silently barreling down the track toward you. You don't see it, you don't hear it. And you don't feel it coming until it is right next you. Then your body is suddenly battered with a frightening force, while the earth itself is shaking violently under your feet. When the train is gone, you can only stand there in stunned silence, wondering what happened. That day at the marina, as the tremor swept through me, I bent over and held my head, turning away from Mikey and trying desperately to control myself. I have no idea what he must have thought or if he noticed anything at all because I could not look at him. How could he not have noticed? He didn't say anything. I was feeling nuts again, and I was trying desperately to act normal. I am tormented wondering why I tried so hard to pretend nothing was happening. What was happening? What was it that sealed my lips? Was it because I thought I had frightened him before when I told him about the dream? I don't know. It was as if the universe was trying to shake some sense into me, hitting me over the head with a two-by-four. It was my last chance, and I didn't heed the message.

We walked quietly together toward the parking lot where we met up with Cristal and Peggie. Peggie had noticed a lipstick-red Toyota Celica in the parking lot and told Mikey that was the car she wanted. He didn't show much enthusiasm, which was uncharacteristic of him. I turned to face Mikey, looked up into his deep blue eyes and gave him a big hug. I said, "Good-bye."

He said, "Good-bye." Neither of us smiled. I felt so preoccupied with what had happened that I forgot to remind him to call me when he got home. It was a family safety rule to check in when we reached our destinations. I watched as he drove away out of the marina. That was the last time I saw him alive.

CHAPTER 9

Day of the Accident

June 15, 1993

I got up late on the morning of June 15, 1993. I remember feeling compelled to take a bike ride that day. It was strange that I had such an urge to go. I took bike rides occasionally, but never felt such urgency. There were some things I needed to do before leaving, but I rushed through them frantically as if I had an appointment to keep. Then I got my biking outfit on, hauled the mountain bike up out of the basement, filled the water bottle, and set out. To get to the park, I had to ride a couple miles through a residential area in town, then over an expressway overpass. Since the overpass was on a narrow uphill road with a lot of traffic, I walked my bike across the bridge section that spanned the highway. Then I jumped back on the bike and sped downhill to the T-intersection at the bottom where there was a stop sign. The crossroad was hilly with heavy, high-speed traffic. I could enter the park through a back entrance there. The park had a bike path wide enough for both bicyclers and walkers. Since it was a Tuesday during work hours, I encountered no one else in the park that day. The path was interesting. It wound around overlapping loops, over gentle hills, past stands of aromatic pines, and beside a prairie of wildflowers. There were shady stretches that offered relief from the sun on hot days, but this day was not hot. It was an ideal day for biking. I rode for a couple of hours and then headed back home. I rode part way up the narrow road to the overpass and got off my bike again to walk over the bridge section. When I got to the far edge of the bridge, a large, heavy truck rumbled by on the roadway beneath, violently shaking the bridge foundation. I felt myself blanch with fear. I had never been frightened by the traffic before, although it was always fast and heavy under the bridge. As the vibration passed through me, I felt a dark shadow fall across my soul. I rode the rest of the way home feeling unsettled.

At home I showered and changed into comfortable clothes. Before I lay down on the couch to watch the five-o'clock news, I thought of giving Mikey a call. He had not reported back that he got home safely from the boat party. That was three days ago, I reasoned. Surely, he was home safely. I felt exhausted, so I didn't call. The fresh air and exercise had tired me, and I dozed off now and then as the evening passed. I was alone in the house as my husband was on the sailboat at the marina. Later in the evening I was awakened by the phone ringing, and I got up to answer it in my office. It was my sister, Sarah. While I was talking to her on the phone I got a call-waiting beep and flashed to answer the incoming call. It was Cristal. It was quite late which made it unusual, but it was also unusual because she never called me. She asked if I was sitting down. Her voice was monotone. I had no idea what to expect. I said "Yes," even though I was standing.

She said, "Mike had an accident. He's up to the funeral home." She said it so matter-of-factly that I was confused.

I said, "What is he doing there?"

"He's dead."

I screamed and hung up the phone, slamming it down as I recoiled in horror from that message. I collapsed to the floor and went crawling into the den, screaming and screaming, "No, no, no, no." I completely wet my slacks. I heard the phone ring again. Only now do I know that it was the call-back ring from my sister's call that was still on hold. I crawled on my hands and knees back to my office, screaming and screaming, and picked up the phone. My sister's voice was asking me what was going on, but I couldn't respond. I laid the phone down on the desk and fell to the floor, still screaming. I then reached back up to the desk and hung up the phone because I didn't want to repeat the horrible news. I crawled back into the dark den still sobbing. When the phone rang again a few minutes later, I crawled back to my office and answered it, still wailing. My sister Nancy was now on the phone. She kept patiently repeating, "You have got to tell us what is happening, Jane." Finally, her calm manner managed to break through my shattered brain. I didn't want to say it. *To say it would make it true.* As Nancy kept gently insisting on an answer, I finally forced out two words, "Mikey" and "dead." She said they were coming to me.

I lay curled up in a fetal position on the floor by my desk, shaking and sobbing uncontrollably when the phone rang again. Thinking it was my sister again, I answered. It was Cristal. I recoiled from her efficient voice. She told me she wanted to call Mike's dad, and she needed the phone number of the marina. In an instant I realized if she delivered the horrible news to him as harshly as she did to me, he would die from a heart attack. I quickly came to my senses and firmly told her not to call him, that I would call him myself. Instinctively, I knew she would not honor my request, so I hurried to make the call first. Fortuitously, I had just gotten the emergency number of the marina the week before and had written it on the calendar on my desk. I don't know why I had decided I might need it, but there it was right by the phone. I dialed it as fast as I could. I told the gatekeeper to please go get my husband, Mike Quint, off the sailboat Edelweiss. It was an emergency. A few minutes later Mike got on the phone. I was sobbing and told him I had something so horrible to tell him that I didn't want to even say it. "Our Mikey had an accident. Our dear son is dead." He started to cry, almost a whimper. Then he said the Indiana State Police were pulling up to the gatehouse and were asking for him. Cristal had sent them to deliver the message anyway. I was thankful I had gotten to him first. He left the marina immediately for Angola, breaking the speed limit the whole way. The state police followed him right up to Mikey's house, but excused him when they found out the reason he was speeding. How he could have driven when under such duress is incomprehensible to me.

Then, in horror, I thought of having to tell Peggie. I quickly called her and was momentarily surprised because she was crying. Cristal had already gotten to her! Anger flared up in me that she had dared to call her while I was calling Mike. Only recently, I'd asked Peggie how Cristal had told her the news. She said she remembered exactly. Cristal had asked her if she was sitting down. Peggie said, "No, why, what's up?"

Cristal said, "We have to make funeral plans for Mike." My God! What kind of person was she? What kind of person tells a sister that her only brother is dead like that? Peggie told me I was screaming and screaming on the phone, but I managed to tell her that Sarah and Nancy were coming to drive us to Angola. We would pick her up at her apartment as fast as possible.

My sisters were coming. Thank God I was on the phone with Sarah when that horrible call came. Thank God they were not far away. I became aware that I was a total mess. My slacks were soaked with urine all down the pant legs. I quickly cleaned up, put fresh clothes on and waited for them to arrive. I had to get to dear Peggie and hold her tight. When we drove up to Peggie's apartment, she was waiting on the front steps in the arms of a friend and crying inconsolably. We collapsed in each other's arms sobbing. She felt like a small helpless child in my arms, so fragile and wounded.

I don't remember how we got to the Indiana Toll Road. My sister Sarah was driving. It was a long ride, but I barely remember any of it. I think Peggie and I were together in the back seat. At some point, Nancy quietly asked me how Mikey had died. I said, "He was hit by a car while riding his bicycle." She sucked in her breath in horror. She herself bicycled. We all did. I don't think anyone spoke again the rest of the trip. At least I don't remember. I do remember the night was so dark. There was no moon. We were riding through the rural countryside with only an occasional farm along the route. Sodium lamps illuminated the outbuildings with an eerie glow.

Some fifteen years later, at my request, my sister Sarah wrote this letter of her recollections of that night.

> Dear Jane,
>
> I was living at Nancy's house, and Nancy and Bruce had gone to bed. I was in my room talking to you on the phone at around 10:30 PM. While we were on the phone you got a "call waiting" beep and told me to hold on while you answered it. I waited briefly and somehow you must have pushed the button, which brought me back on line. All I could hear was the most blood-curdling, sorrowful, wailing, primal scream that I had ever heard. I will never forget it. It was terrifying. I didn't know

what was happening to you. Was there someone in the house attacking you? I was frozen to the phone, listening as hard as I could to try to figure out what was going on. I continued to hear you, but then the phone was disconnected.

I went downstairs and softly knocked on Nancy's bedroom door. She responded, "Come in." I walked into the room, and in the dark told her that something happened while I was talking to you on the phone and you were wailing and screaming. I didn't know exactly what had happened, but knew we had to get to you. So, Nancy called you back. When you answered the phone, you were still crying uncontrollably.

Nancy repeatedly asked in a very low, calm voice, "You have got to tell us what is happening, Jane."

Your reply shocked us in its abruptness and finality: "Mikey. Dead." Nancy and I left to drive to your house immediately. I couldn't get there fast enough. As I think back, that trip was like a blurred streak of movement as if a camera were riding in a car next to us recording ... now arriving ... rushing into your house ... hearing your sobs ... rushing to hold you.

I drove you to Batavia to pick up Peggie. In the car, sobbing, you started telling me more details. You kept saying, "This isn't the way it's supposed to happen. A child isn't supposed to die before the parent." I couldn't find any words to console you. I felt helpless. I don't remember the sequence of events at Peggie's apartment. Somehow, the four of us all got into my car and drove to Angola. I think by the time we got there it was getting light outside, because I remember the four of us, Mike, Mikey's wife, and maybe someone else, met up in the middle of the front yard and formed a tight circle holding each other and crying. I remember going into the house, more talking, endless hours of "what to do next." At some point, Nancy and I left to drive back home to Illinois. I can't remember anything else until the funeral.

Stunning snapshots of that period of time pop into my mind. It was all so very sad.

Love,

Sarah

CHAPTER 10

Scene of the Accident

Mikey was indeed, "up to the funeral home." That was a peculiar country euphemism I had never heard before. We went to the funeral home and spoke to the funeral director. He was very compassionate and took his time with us. When I asked what killed Mikey he quietly told us his neck was broken. He was struck head-on by a car while he was riding his bicycle. Head-on? How could that be? He had a puncture wound in his chest, his ribs were broken, and his leg was broken. I wanted to see him, but was told he wasn't "ready" yet. Apparently Cristal had seen him earlier, probably to identify him. She said she had not seen any external signs of injury, just a trickle of blood from his right ear. I answered all the questions for the obituary. Together we picked out a beautiful oak casket, because he loved working with wood. Cristal took care of the visitation that was to take place in Angola. We would then take him back to Munster for the funeral. He would be laid to rest in the cemetery where his grandpa was buried. I shall always be grateful that Cristal let him come home where we could visit his grave.

Looking down to the T-Intersection

The scene of the accident was close to his house. His bike odometer had stopped at 2.6 miles. We drove the path he took that fateful day. It was a quiet country road that led through a residential area to an expressway overpass, curved past an old white farmhouse, and then down a steep hill to a T-intersection at the bottom where there was a stop sign. The crossroad was hilly with heavy, high-speed traffic. There were farm fields on all three corners, but the corn was not high enough to obstruct the view. I could not understand how that driver did not see him, or how he did not see the car. There may have been a moment when the hill on the crossroad to his right side blocked his vision of the car just cresting the hill, but only a split moment. There was loose fine gravel at the bottom of the hill, which may have caused a skid. We could not imagine what had caused the accident.

We stood on the side of the country road where the collision occurred. Witnesses say Mikey did not stop at the stop sign and turned right into the path of the oncoming car, which was traveling at a high rate of speed. The car had tried to stop, leaving a burnout on the roadway and digging its front wheel into the umber-colored soil next to the gray asphalt road. Mikey hit the windshield of the car, catapulted into the air, hit the metal pole of the street sign, and landed where the shoulder of the road sloped deeply into a grassy ditch. We could see the indentation where his body had landed on the soft earth. I recorded that exact spot in my mind. The parts of the mangled bicycle had been removed, but I saw his shoes were still lying in the road. I picked them up and hugged them to my body and took them home with me. I picked up the pieces of his shattered helmet which were strewn all along the side of the road. On one piece of his helmet I noticed a small red triangle and discovered that he had put his name and address in an emergency slot there. I remembered his telling me about that safety feature of his helmet. Unfortunately, no one found it at the time of the accident. That is why it took so long for him to be identified and for us to get the news. Mikey was a meticulous planner. He had even planned for this emergency.

At the county sheriff's office, I read the police report given by the driver of the car that killed Mikey:

> I was going about fifty-five mph when I saw the bicyclist coming fast down Buck Lake Road. I slammed on my breaks as soon as I saw him. I tried to stop, but I wasn't quick enough. I also tried to swerve toward the ditch and then the other way because he was swerving all over the road. I don't think he could stop because he was going so fast. The bicyclist had an expression on his face like he knew it was going to happen. When he hit me, he hit the right front of my car. I saw him fly in the air into my windshield and the bike broke into pieces. I started screaming. The black car behind me was already stopped and she was out of the car. I was screaming and crying to her and she told me it wasn't my fault. She saw me try to stop and she saw him flying down the hill, swerving and coming straight toward me. Then the old lady up the hill came running down saying she had called the police.

I was astounded that she said "he'd hit her"! A bike has no chance against a car. It is absurd to me that the rules of the road apply equally to cars and bikes. The sheriff said she was extremely shook up. I hissed angrily, "She is alive." Was I supposed to feel pity for her because killing my son upset her day? The sheriff said Mikey drove into the path of her car. I said the driver should have driven defensively. I couldn't see her side of the story at all. I was insulted to learn they ran an alcohol test on him. "Why not on the driver?" I asked. No answer. Of course, he was clean. He had been clean for five years! How ironic that all the times he was DUI, he was killed when he was sober.

The driver has probably now forgotten the day she killed a promising young man, a beloved only son, an only sibling, a newly married husband. She was an inexperienced teenager. She probably has never realized all the lives that were ruined because she was driving too fast and couldn't stop for an unexpected event. I didn't want to know her name at the time. I've never wanted to know anything about her life since. Apparently, she called Cristal and asked if she should come to the visitation. Cristal told her "No." and I am glad because I did not want her face to haunt my dreams. But, maybe she should have come and hid at the back of the funeral parlor to witness the devastation she'd caused. I wonder if she is married now with cherished children of her own. If so, I am sure she would pray they would not be run down like wild animals should they make a mistake and run into the road. "It wasn't my fault." How pathetic! If she hadn't been driving so fast, maybe she could have avoided hitting a biker who was obviously in trouble. Maybe the chain broke on his bicycle and he couldn't stop. Maybe he skidded on the loose gravel. She was going too fast and there was no room for error. I trust her nightmares have long subsided. We have never recovered.

As I read the report again I noted that she did not run to him after he was hit. She sought comfort for herself instead. Another driver who witnessed the accident stopped her car and ran to him as he lay in the grassy ditch. She said he was not breathing. When she asked his name, she got no response. He then started to breathe steadily. The funeral director said he may have lived five minutes. I often think of that anonymous woman and how grateful I am that she was beside my son and spoke to him and held his hand as he lay dying. At least he was not alone.

Emergency team tending Mikey at accident scene

The next day, the *Evening Star* newspaper ran a front-page story with the headline:

Collision Kills Rural Angola Bicyclist

Angola—Steuben County man died about 4:45 PM Tuesday after his bicycle was struck by a car. Michael Quint, 33, of rural Angola, died of multiple internal injuries and a broken neck. He was pronounced dead at the scene.

Quint rode into the path of the car, and the driver was unable to avoid striking his bike, the County Sheriff's Department said.

The roadway is narrow and hilly near the scene. Rescuers found him face-down in a grassy ditch just beyond the T of the intersection. His bike remained on the roadway, its metal shape unrecognizable except for the wheels.

The car faced northwest beyond the point of impact, its windshield shattered. The driver held her face in her hands and shook uncontrollably.

We went to the place where the car had been towed. I was astonished that an insurance agent was already there writing up a damage estimate. Was fixing the car such a top priority? My son had not even been prepared for burial yet. I bitterly wondered what the replacement cost of the windshield smeared with my son's blood would be. My son could not be replaced at any cost. How could the routine of life continue when our world ended? When I looked at the car I was shocked. It had an indentation on the hood, and the windshield was shattered. I immediately remembered those mysterious loud sounds I heard in my house: da–DA, da–DA, da–DA. I gasped when I realized that was exactly the sound of his body first hitting the hood and then the windshield. I felt dizzy realizing it was around the same time of day as his accident. An old wives' tale I heard as a child echoed in my head: Death knocks three times. "Oh my God," I cried in anguish. How could I be so stupid, but how could I have possibly known what those sounds foretold?

The police report listed the time of the accident as 4:43 PM EDT. I recalled that I almost telephoned him that day after my bike ride. My mind tried to frantically calculate what time I had thought of calling him. Was it before he left for his bike ride? Could I have saved him if only I had called? Why didn't I call like I always did? Could I have delayed his ride enough to change his fate? Guilt flooded over me. It took me some months to realize that Angola was on a different time in the summer than we were in Illinois. In June it would have been 3:43 CDT our time. I realized then that I was riding my bike at the same time Mikey was riding his bike. I had felt compelled to take a bike ride. I learned later that Mikey had left work early to take his bike ride. I took comfort in knowing that we were riding together. Then I recalled that moment when a dark shadow crossed by soul as I crossed the overpass on the highway and felt the bridge shake violently. I shall always believe that is the moment he was struck by the car. My soul shuddered at the moment that my dear son was killed. Why couldn't it have been me instead? I would have gladly died in his place. I should be the one who is dead! Not him! Not him!

CHAPTER 11

Wake in Angola

My husband, daughter, and I must have driven back to Illinois to get appropriate clothes for the visitation in Angola. We must have gone home because I remember getting a phone call from the Naperville body shop that had been repairing and detailing my car. I was cheerfully told that my car was now ready for pick-up that very day. After I hung up, the realization hit me with a vengeance. Of course! The perfect car for a funeral! My classic, black, dignified Mercedes was now repaired, shined and polished just in time for the appointed day. I gasped as I made the connection. That was why I was suddenly compelled to get it fixed! How could I not recognize what I was doing! I was acting as if I subconsciously knew I would need it for a funeral, as if I knew my son was going to die. I was furious at my incredible stupidity! When my husband asked me which car we should take for the funeral, I spitefully refused to take the black Mercedes. It was symbol of my complicity in his death.

I remember little of the visitation in Angola. I remember seeing my Mikey lying in the casket across the room as we entered the funeral parlor. I dragged myself toward him, shaking as if I were a condemned woman going to her execution. I didn't want to see him like that, but I had to. I saw he was dressed in the navy pin-striped suit I had bought him for job interviews after he graduated from college. I was surprised to see his tie. It was one I had bought him for Christmas many years before. I remember that he looked shocked when he opened my gift and saw the tie. I thought he didn't like it and assured him it would not hurt my feelings in the least if he wanted me to exchange it. He insisted he did like it and kept it. I had never seen him wear it, until now. Now I was the one who was shocked at seeing it.

His body looked so strange and rigid. It was a corpse. How I hated using that term for my beloved son. A corpse! How cold and inhuman that word is. I looked at those hands. Yes, they were his strong masculine hands, even bigger than his dad's hands, but they looked so strange. Like a wax model of his hands. How could this really be him? It wasn't him! I couldn't look very long, so I sat on a small couch near the coffin, but not facing it. I looked at him every now and then to let it slowly sink in. I wept the whole time I was sitting there. I hadn't stopped crying since I had gotten that phone call the evening of June 15. I had cried so much my eyes were swollen nearly shut. My voice was so hoarse I could barely talk. I cried and cried and cried. Sometimes only a soft whimper, but I just could not stop crying.

There were so many people there I did not know. Some were Cristal's family who I'd never met. Cristal had two younger sisters who were both married with small children. One of the sisters sat on the small couch opposite me for a while. At first she was as stoic as Cristal, but sitting there watching me cry finally brought a tear to her eye. She then quietly moved away. I assumed that many people there were Mikey's coworkers and his other friends. I believe Mikey's boss praised him to us as an outstanding employee who was obsessed with perfection. Cristal's father was compassionate. He sadly told us he had planned to start biking with Mikey. I wondered if things might have been different if he had. Most people didn't speak to us because they didn't know who we were or maybe they didn't know what to say. One man came and knelt by me as I sat on the couch weeping. He introduced himself, but I don't remember his name. He had a kind face and gentle manner. He may have been the pastor of the church Mikey had attended during his AA sessions. He knew about Mikey's accident almost exactly five years earlier that led to his spiritual epiphany and recovery from alcoholism. In an effort to comfort me he said, "God gave him five more years." I was instantly enraged. I was supposed to appreciate that God gave him five more years? Why not ten, or twenty, or fifty more years! Why wait till he had cleaned up his life, given up drinking and smoking, married, and settled down, then boom … that's it buddy. The idea made me so angry the man must have realized it and sadly withdrew. I could see he was not judgmental. He saw my misery was inconsolable.

I silently fumed as I pondered this concept of God, who in "His mysterious ways His wonder doth perform," or whatever the absurd excuse for irrational injustice was. It was a cruel God who didn't listen to a mother's prayers or care that the world needed a talented young man. God didn't need him. We needed him! I needed him! Yet, I didn't actually blame God because I didn't believe that God had anything to do with Mikey's accident. The truth was, God didn't cause it, and God also didn't prevent it. God was irrelevant. If I didn't hate God it was only because I didn't believe in God. I was doubtful before, now I was sure there was no God. We have only each other in this world. I had counted on Mikey to be there in our old age. I counted on adoring my grandchildren and watching Mikey blossom as a father. Now, he was gone. Our future was gone. With jaded eyes I watched Cristal's mother callously dolling out the floral arrangements to her family and friends. She didn't offer any to me. I didn't want any. I wanted my son back.

CHAPTER 12

Funeral in Munster

It rained all day long as Mikey's body was carried back home to Munster. The downpour continued into the night. It rained and rained and rained, and just like my tears, it wouldn't stop. My sister Carole stayed beside us that evening in the hotel room to comfort us. She said that the heavens were pouring out their grief at the loss of a great soul. She believed evil forces in this world conspired to kill Mikey because he was so loved. Many years later Carole still remembered when she first saw us after he died:

> It seemed like an eternity passed before I could see both of you. I needed to be near you. What I witnessed at the first sight of you was a bloody, raw, unchecked pain coming from two people I loved and cared for deeply. The pain was all around you, stabbing at you from every angle, tearing you apart, killing you. Our beautiful Mikey was dead! My God! It could not be! It's hard to go back to that time.

The rains finally subsided by the time of the funeral the next morning, but there was still a fine, cool mist in the air. At the funeral parlor we met with the new reverend from the Hyde Park Methodist church where Mikey and Peggie were baptized so long ago. She spoke to Cristal and me to get information for the eulogy asking us, "Do you want a short service or long?"

Cristal quickly said, "Short."

I was surprised. I said, "No, no, no, not short!" That was the first inkling I had of how differently we grieved. Cristal wanted to cut everything off so she wouldn't feel the pain. I wanted to cling onto everything because it was too painful to let go.

I remember when Carole wheeled my mother into the funeral home that morning. Mother looked all crumpled down in her wheelchair. Her pain was so obvious. She said, "I didn't want him to die. I am old. Why couldn't it have been me?" She was crying. I had never seen my mother cry. Then she took my hand and told me, "This is the last time you will see him." I hadn't really thought about that. I would never see him again? I kept going up to the coffin and looking at his face, touching his beautiful, strong hands and kissing him on the cheek. I remember thinking I should have been the one to wash his body to prepare it for burial, like women did in days long ago. I wondered why people let strangers do that now. I was his mother; I bathed him as a small child before I put him to bed. Shouldn't I have been the one to bathe him for his final rest? Now he was so cold to my touch. I could see he was blue under the makeup. I could faintly smell the masked odor, but I still didn't want to bury him. I didn't want to let him go.

Peggie was offended that Cristal had removed his simple gold wedding band. "Why couldn't she let him keep it?" she asked me. I could think of no reason.

The service was long and the remembrances often humorous as family members gave their eulogies. Cousin Lizzie remembered a time when we were visiting their house in Crown Point when they were all children. All the kids thought it would be great fun to untie the bales of hay the farmer next door had just harvested. The farmer didn't find out until Mikey and Peggie had already gone home, so they escaped the spankings meted out to the rest of them. Cousin Karen remembered when she and Mikey searched for marbles in the Porter Middle School field and found hundreds of them. She wished she could turn back the clock. Cousin Diana spoke about how they were both Purdue engineers. Peggie began reading a beautiful tribute she had written, but could only read a few lines. Aunt Carole read the rest of her tribute for her. In *A Sister's Promise*, which is included in full at the end of the book, Peggie recounted all the wonderful memories she had growing up with Mikey, her older brother and only sibling. They were close in age and were inseparable. She idolized him and wanted to be just like him, even when he called her a copycat. People smiled at the charming childhood memories, like fitting in the trunk of a Volkswagen Beetle together and hearing Santa's sleigh bells one Christmas Eve. As teenagers, the memories were of going to rock concerts and football games at Purdue. Peggie said she could always count on Mikey to be there for her. As young adults she remembered that he put his heart and soul into everything he did. She promised to remember his laughter, his smile, his beautiful laughing eyes, his strength, and his courage. She made a promise to him to live life to the fullest as he always did. To be his eyes, his ears, his senses, and to enjoy the world for him.

> I love you forever, my dear brother, Mike! You shall never be forgotten. Never!

I also could not read the tribute I had written to my summer child. My sister Sarah read it for me. She said I just cried and cried and cried, but she still saw the appreciation I felt for those who took time to speak about him, those who did not want the service to be short. No one in Cristal's family spoke. I was surprised they had nothing to say about their daughter's husband, not even to us personally.

I don't remember how the funeral arrangements were made. My sisters Sarah and Nancy had purchased the cemetery plots in the same cemetery where Grandpa was buried. They put a pen in my hand to sign a check for them. Were they actually concerned they would not get paid back? My sister Clarissa asked me if she could speak to Cristal about financial planning. Was she actually drumming up business at a time like this? Such concerns were incomprehensible to me. Sarah collected the names from the floral arrangements so I could write thank-you notes later. She chose the peace plant for me to take home. So many people were there. I remember being so pleased that his high school swimming coach had remembered him after all those years. Peggie's friend who knew Mikey only a short time told me he had a dream of Mikey swimming in the ocean with the dolphins. I smiled, thinking that is exactly what he would do. My brother-in-law Bruce warmed my heart when he said, "You were a good mother." No one could have said words that meant more to me. I showed him the necklace with a purple quartz heart I was wearing, and said I had a purple heart like a soldier wounded in battle. He didn't understand what I meant and wanted to argue the point. In the end, it was my sisters who guided us through our tragedy. They carried the burden when we were too weak to do so; they held us in their arms when we could barely stand; they spoke for us when we could not; they eased our excruciating pain with their kindness. Without them, I doubt that we would have survived. I shall always be grateful.

As the funeral procession assembled, we were in the immediate-family limousine directly behind the hearse that carried Mikey's body. Mike, Peggie, and I sat together in the front row of seats while Cristal and her parents sat behind us. While we waited for everyone to get in their cars for the procession to the cemetery, Cristal's mother started complaining that her other kids were too far back in the lineup. I was incredulous at her insensitivity and wanted to scream at her, "Would you like them to change places with my son in the front of the line?" She may have noticed my reaction, because she was quiet for a while. Then she started chattering away about a special diet she was trying out. I could not stand it and put my fingers in my ears to shut her voice out. I didn't care if she saw me. What kind of mother was she that she couldn't understand the loss of a child? I felt trapped in the car and wanted so desperately to get away from her. Her lack of empathy was painful. As we pulled away and drove through Munster, Cristal's dad asked if this was where Mikey grew up. I was happy to point out where he went to high school and some other landmarks along the route. His interest in Mikey comforted me. He was a warm compassionate person—so different from his wife.

I have tried hard to remember exactly who the pallbearers were, but I cannot bring that image to mind. I do remember noting that they were Mikey's six male cousins: five by blood and one by marriage. I've had to ask the cousins themselves. Three were Jimmy, Eddie, and Peter, my sisters' boys. I believe the cousin by blood was Karen's husband, Rick. I remember finding comfort that such loving hands carried Mikey to the small chapel on the cemetery grounds. Sarah, whose son Peter was among them, said their young faces looked so sad, so somber, as they carried their loving cousin to his grave in disbelief. After the consecration, we each took a red rose from his casket bouquet. Mikey was laid to rest under a stately sycamore tree in the Garden of Devotion. I later designed a headstone for him with a Purdue emblem I found in the desk he had refinished. I chose a stanza from the poem "And You As Well Must Die, Beloved Dust" by Edna St. Vincent Millay. It described so eloquently how I felt:

> Nor shall my love avail you in your hour.
> In spite of all my love, you will arise
> Upon that day and wander down the air
> Obscurely as the unattended flower,
> It mattering not how beautiful you were,
> Or how beloved above all else that dies.

I then added the words, "Until we meet again." It was Saturday, June 19, 1993. That was the last time I saw him.

CHAPTER 13

Afterward

After the funeral, Mike, Peggie and I drove every weekend to Mikey's house in Angola. We needed to be there because we couldn't believe he was actually gone, and we thought Cristal needed our emotional support. Her family lived some distance away and was never there at any time we were there. The house felt so empty without his exuberant presence. We wandered around lost in our grief, wondering what to do.

I looked for the irises that he had so proudly shown me a few weeks earlier. They had died, and I plucked off their dead heads. A bed of zinnias he had planted from seeds we had given him from our garden came up as the weeks passed. I was perplexed that they were all white. There had been no white zinnias among ours. In fact, I had never even seen a white zinnia. Every single one of these was white. Other flowers in his yard also came up white. It struck me as spiritual symbolism that I couldn't quite comprehend. At night I slept in the spare bedroom that faced toward a stand of tall popular trees skirting the back of his yard. Every night for one week the trees glittered with thousands of flashing lightning bugs. I had never seen so many lightning bugs in one place at one time. It was as if the Milky Way had dipped down from the heavens and draped a diaphanous sash of twinkling stars across the trees. It was breathtaking. I gazed at it for hours and again felt a spiritual connection to Mikey. I wondered if he was showing me the beauty of the spiritual world.

His garden began to grow. It seemed strange to me how the seeds he had planted were now coming to life after his death. Peggie would often sit in his garden because she could feel his presence there. His study of organic gardening was apparent. There was a rock shelter for a toad that would eat insects and a border of marigolds that would repel deer. There was a chicken wire fence to keep rabbits out; its gate opened on the now completed pathway of yellow bricks. I loved the tiny purple flower of the summer savory. I crushed the leaves between my fingers and found comfort in the aroma. As the summer progressed, the garden went untended, the vegetables largely unused. Most of the ample crop of tomatoes rotted on the vine. I took some sage home for use at future Thanksgivings. Peggie harvested the hot jalapeño peppers. She donated them to a memorial chili dinner for a young man who had drowned in the Fox River later that summer. His name also was Mike.

Peggie in Mikey's garden

I am glad we got along with Cristal those first weeks. One of the first things she did was give me the present Mikey had already bought for my August birthday. It was a coffee mug decorated with party balloons that said "Happy Birthday." She said when he picked it out he proclaimed, "Mom would love this!" He was more right than he could have imagined. Slowly she revealed some things that happened around the time he died. She said Mikey had explained embalming to her a couple weeks before he died. I was stunned to learn that. Why was he talking about embalming? Did he also have a premonition that he was going to die? She told us that a medical report arrived in the mail the day after he died. It showed that his sperm count was fine. They apparently were seeking help because she was having difficulty getting pregnant. I remembered that I once had the feeling I would never have a grandchild from him. When she mentioned that they had been together for eight years, I was more than surprised. I really didn't know much about her during those years.

She spoke of the many vacations they went on together. "I never was anywhere before I met Mike," she said. "He took me to so many places around the country." She was mourning the loss of their dreams together. "We'd just started," she said. "It's not fair."

They both worked at the same manufacturing plant. She said the first day she went back to work after the funeral, the shop lights flickered on and off as she walked across the plant floor. She said Mikey used to do that all the time to get her attention. Everyone in the shop was perplexed by it. They finally decided it must have been an electrical malfunction. I wondered. She began to be frightened at night because she said she heard him breathing in bed beside her. It scared her so that she couldn't stay there alone at night anymore. One afternoon, when I was sitting in the dining room, I saw a movement in Mikey's office. Out of the corner of my eye I thought I saw a white amorphous shape move quickly across the doorway and vanish into the wall. I got up to see if Peggie or Cristal were in his office. They were not. I looked out the window and saw both of them in the front yard. I tried to make sense of it. The idea of an apparition crept into my thoughts, but I pushed it away. Maybe, it was a reflection of the sun off a passing car. As I sat back down in the dining room I sadly wondered if Mikey's spirit had briefly returned to his office.

These strange occurrences didn't frighten me, but they made me worry that his soul was troubled. I'd heard of souls that do not know they were dead wandering confused on the earthly plane. Could this be happening because his death was so sudden? I knew how much he hated leaving home abruptly. I was tormented by the thought that he was lost and alone in darkness. I started to pray that day. I fervently whispered a mother's prayer over and over, a hundred, a thousand times, just like I'd done all the years he was growing up. As I prayed for his soul to find peace, a fragment of a prayer I must have heard long ago in church welled up from the depths of my despair:

> May the Lord bless you and keep you;
> May the Lord make His face shine upon you,
> And be gracious unto you;
> May the Lord lift up His countenance upon you,
> And give you peace.

CHAPTER 14

People Grieve Differently

I don't know exactly when Cristal's attitude changed toward us. Perhaps the initial shock had finally worn off and grim reality was setting in for her. Her sadness changed to anger. She seemed angry at Mikey for leaving her and destroying their dreams. I began to realize that our presence there was constant reminder of him and all that was lost. We became the target of her anger, but the worst of it was directed at me, his mother.

I first became aware of her hostility the day I walked in the house and saw stacks of boxes packed full of Mikey's clothes. She was getting them ready to donate to the Goodwill. I said, "I would like to keep a few of his clothes."

She sarcastically remarked, "Oh, are you going to make a shrine for him?" Her voice was snotty. I was stunned. That is the first time anyone had intentionally aimed to hurt me during this whole painful ordeal. I stuttered when I said I just wanted a few of his things to help me through this. She stopped what she was doing and abruptly went into his closet and took a handful of ironed dress shirts, blue jeans, and slacks all on hangers and practically threw them at me. She was giving the stuff away to strangers. What was the problem in giving some of his clothing to me if I wanted it? For whatever reason

I wanted it? Why should I have to justify wanting it? I was chagrined, but I gathered up his clothes and kept them. Then I thought, "How dare she!" I asked for a box of his T-shirts she had already packed up. They were from Purdue, the Grand Canyon, the Apostle Islands, Lake Placid, Florida, and other places he had visited over the years. She obviously didn't want them, and I knew Peggie would love to wear them. I took them immediately out to my car, out of her clutches.

Mike thinks her anger toward me started when I was looking through Mikey's desk for the new Purdue emblem so that I could have it engraved on his headstone. Cristal had given no thought to a headstone. The emblem had changed since I had gone to Purdue, and I wanted to find the new design. Cristal's face was contorted in anger as she accused me of riffling through their things and making lists of stuff I wanted. I was astonished! Making lists? That didn't even make sense. I showed her the Purdue emblem I had found, but she was not convinced. I felt humiliated once again. I rationalized her bizarre behavior by telling myself she was grieving and lashing out at us because we were there in front of her. Her agony was apparent. She had quit eating and was nearly a skeleton by that time. When I complained about the false accusation to my husband he explained, "She never liked you." He had a way of being brutally honest. Despite my efforts to welcome her and make her feel comfortable, I often felt she cast me in the stereotypical role of the despised mother-in-law.

Peggie was incensed at the idea that Cristal didn't like me. "You were always very good to her. She was just standoffish. She couldn't warm up to anyone!"

Still, it bothered me, and I finally asked my husband, "Why didn't she like me?"

He thought for a moment and said, "Because you and Mikey were so close." I remember Mikey had told me Cristal didn't get along with her mother. Perhaps, she resented his closeness to me, but he was dead now. Why begrudge us that anymore?

I decided to overlook her insensitive behavior because we were all grieving. One day I asked her if I could have Mikey's drafting table. "No," she gloated, "that belongs to the company, and it has to go back to them." I wondered if the company might be willing to sell it. It was worth a try.

I called his boss to ask if I could purchase the table. He sounded sad when he said, "You may have it." Cristal was enraged that I had gone around her to get it! That is when she started telling people at work that Mikey's family was only interested in money.

When I told my husband that, he was incredulous. "Money—what money? We didn't ask for a cent!" We could have made a claim because Mikey had died without a will. We had told her we didn't want any money and had already signed legal papers releasing any claim. We were financially comfortable. I didn't say so, but money from our son's death would have been blood money to us. Her slander offended and disgusted me. This time she had gone too far.

I struck back, "You are the only one who will profit financially from Mikey's death!"

Instead of realizing how she had offended us, she lashed out at me. "You have no idea what I am going through to say something like that!" Well, it was the truth. My sister, Clarissa, who had gained Cristal as a client at Mikey's funeral, was handling Cristal's finances. I had decided to overlook my sister's opportunism because she was convinced she was providing a needed service to Cristal. Besides, I learned things I would not have known otherwise. My sister told me that Cristal had gotten a large life insurance settlement. In fact, a few weeks before he died, Mikey had changed his policy to double the payout in case of accidental death. My heart sank when I heard that, because I wondered if he subconsciously knew he was going to die, as I subconsciously knew. Then I recalled another instance of her callous behavior. The day after Mikey was killed, Cristal was on the phone putting in an insurance claim for the mangled Trek bicycle that he had been riding when he was killed. And she was accusing us of being focused on money?

Psychologists would say she was projecting her money concerns on us, but I was not going to make any more excuses for her. She didn't have an inkling of what Mikey meant to us. She certainly had no idea of what we were going through, either. I tried to tell her how we felt losing a child and how Peggie felt losing her only sibling, but she stared at me blankly. She couldn't empathize with us, and I couldn't deal with her attacks anymore. It was just too painful. I decided then that I had to get away from her. She was just like her mother.

We stopped going to the house in Angola and turned the matter over to our lawyer for settlement. We had turned down money but wanted some of Mikey's personal things. And I intended to have them. It took nearly a year of wrangling with her for just for that! At some point my lawyer asked me what was wrong with her. She acted crazy. I began to wonder if she was having a nervous breakdown. She kept changing her mind about things she already agreed we could have. "I've decided you can't have the desk he refinished after all," she said. I told our lawyer the history of that desk and insisted on having it. My husband would have loved having some of Mikey's new woodworking tools, but she wouldn't permit it. She gave them instead to her brothers-in-law who never knew Mikey. I began to feel that she was punishing us for the pain Mikey caused her by dying.

She told my sister during one financial planning visit, "They didn't lose nothin'!"

My sister was stunned and simply replied, "They've lost their only son." Her understanding father must have reasoned with Cristal by telling her that all we wanted were the things he left home with. In the end, all we got were the things he packed up on that snowy January day in 1985 to start his new life in Angola. It was enough. The painful battle was finally over—or so I thought.

We drove to Angola on a hot summer day in 1994 to pick up the items Cristal agreed we could have. It was a long, hot ride, but when we got to the house Cristal was not there. She had dumped all the items in a big pile in the middle of the garage and had locked up the house as if we were going to steal something. I had hoped to see the inside of his house one last time. That was not to be. We couldn't even get a drink of water. It was humiliating to have to go to a gas station in town to use the restrooms. Fortunately, Mikey's good friends Eric and Cara arrived to help us load the things up in our vehicle. We could not have done it without them. They thoughtfully brought a cooler of drinks and refreshments. Their friendship was a true blessing. I will always be grateful for them.

If Mikey had ever guessed Cristal would be the kind of person who would treat his parents and sister with such meanness, he would never have married her. I believe she loved him in her own way, but she did not understand how much he loved his family. He would have never forgiven her for what she did that day. Whenever I hear that banal expression that people grieve differently, I think of Cristal. It is certainly true. Yet, the way you grieve reveals something of your character and your soul. Her unrelenting maltreatment of the family of the husband she claimed to love revealed a cold heart. We didn't see her that day, or ever again. It was a sad way to end.

Peggie and I at Mikey's cross by the road

For the next several years, on June 15th, Mike, Peggie, and I journeyed back to Angola to the roadside where Mikey was killed. Mike made a large white cross which he pounded into the ground at the exact spot where Mikey fell after he was hit. Peggie painted his name on the cross. I tied flowers and patriotic ribbons on it. As we sat there in the grass, it was not unusual for a passing motorist to stop to ask if we needed help. One young man who stopped was a musician who gave us a tape of spiritual music he had recorded. The cassette was called *The Journey*. One of the songs on it was "Whatever Happens is Best." Another year we found a note in a plastic baggie tied to the cross. It was from Cara and Eric. They had lost our phone number and hoped we would contact them. We did and visited them at their home. They had adopted a second child, another daughter.

The last time we made our pilgrimage the cross had been moved. I shuddered when I saw it high up on the opposite hill propped against the farmer's barbed wire fence. It looked like a crucifixion cross looming over the accident scene. Then I noticed a pair of lovers' initials on the back of the stop sign at the intersection. Cristal had brought her new boyfriend to this hallowed place where Mikey had died. They had marked their initials inside a heart on the back of the stop sign there. A chill ran through me. I knew intuitively that the intent was to taunt Mikey and to torment us. It felt evil. If I could find any silver lining in this twisted aftermath, it was that Mikey was no longer married to her. I was glad he was not buried with his wedding band. He was free. I also sadly had to admit that it was probably best there were no grandchildren. I decided that day I would never return to Angola again.

Mikey's cross up on hill

As time passed, I tried to let go of my bitterness toward Cristal. I never really knew her before Mikey died. There was no formal wedding for us to get to know her family. It was such a short marriage that she didn't get to know us very well. Then we were thrown together under the worst circumstance. I decided to remember that Cristal had a positive influence on Mikey's life. She supported him as he went through Alcoholics Anonymous. She wanted to raise a family with him. She was the only daughter-in-law I would ever have. When Mikey died, she said she would never find anyone else of the same caliber. She bought a cemetery plot for herself next to him where she wanted to be buried, unless she married again. I reached out to Cristal a couple years later. My sister Clarissa had helped her set up a Purdue Scholarship Fund in Mikey's memory with part of his life insurance money. I sent her a bouquet of red roses to thank her and show her that we all still cared, but I got no response. She apparently had no problem leaving things as they were. Peggie described the wall Cristal kept around herself. "She didn't want to get to know us, and she certainly didn't open herself up so we could get to know her. She closed us out from the beginning. In the end she closed us out of Mikey's house." So, I avoid thinking of Cristal to avoid feeling pain I cannot resolve. I did not want to be told the news that she eventually married again. I did not want to know how she was rebuilding her life when it was too late for us. They say that grief will either bring you closer together or tear you apart. It tore us apart from Cristal forever.

CHAPTER 15

Accident Reconstruction

Our journey through grief began after we laid our beloved son to rest in the Garden of Devotion. Numbed with shock, we went back home to Naperville, Illinois. We endured the crucible and had somehow survived. When our neighbor saw us he simply said, "It's so terrible, I don't know what to say." What is there to say? I always said losing a child would kill me, so I couldn't understand why I was still breathing. I knew it was only because of my family. They kept us from being swept away in the undertow of anguish into the abyss. So many loving people shared our burden because they also loved Mikey.

They also were stunned at the loss of such a promising life at its prime. "Such a nice boy. What a shame." Now the funeral was over. Everyone had gone home. People went back to their everyday lives. As we sat alone in our silent home, the emptiness marked by the echo of the ticking grandfather clock, we were perplexed that Mikey was still dead. Was he never coming back? I tried to comprehend those words, "never coming back." How could such a vibrant energy just vanish? Where did he go? And why? What happened that day?

I needed answers. The first question was what caused the accident. In July, 1993, we retained Packer Engineering to conduct an accident-reconstruction investigation. When the three-month investigation was complete, we met with the engineers personally at their business location. Ironically, it was along the very road that led to the park where I rode my bike that fateful day. They were very kind to us. After all these years I still remember their saying I was gracious upon hearing their findings. The accident resulted from Mikey losing control of his bicycle while making a right turn at the T-intersection and traveling into the oncoming lane of traffic. The accident was as the witnesses had reported. We took home a written report that I only scanned at the time. My mind was too shattered to focus on anything.

Many years later when I picked up their report, I was struck by the effort, thoroughness, and scientific expertise involved in reconstructing the accident. I smiled to myself, because Mikey would have approved of their engineering analysis and the detailed documents. Mikey himself liked to record everything he did, from vacation itineraries to garden plant layouts to Civil War troop marches. This was his kind of stuff. After nearly sixteen years I could finally read it completely.

Packer Engineering began by inspecting his new Trek 1200 fourteen-speed touring bicycle. The bicycle had not been struck head-on; rather it was struck on the right side at an angle between forty-five and ninety degrees. The bicycle broke into two pieces, front and rear. All components were examined by a metallurgist. The front and rear brakes appear to have been in good working condition just prior to the accident. There were no defects in the derailleur or gear system. From the position of the jammed lever, it was determined that the bike was in thirteenth gear at the time of the accident (one being the low/slow gear and fourteen being high/fast gear). No design or manufacturing defects were found in the bicycle.

Packer conducted a site inspection on August 24, 1993. A gouge was found in the roadway that corresponded to a section of the bicycle's front sprocket teeth that had been worn down. A stone, with a shiny smear mark, was removed from the gouged area and analyzed in a scanning electron microscope and found to be aluminum—the same composition as the teeth of the front sprocket. The gouge in the road was determined to be the point of initial impact.

Using many data points—including the gouge, the skid marks from the car, and the estimated speed of the bicycle determined from trial runs—Packer reconstructed the accident on a computer. Instantaneously, data was computed showing distances and speeds: of the car as it crested the hill, the point at which the cyclist deviated from his intended path, when the driver perceived the cyclist and began braking, and finally when the cyclist perceived the danger and tried to make it to the other side of the road. Packer concluded that the driver's perception and reaction appeared prompt and reasonable.

The engineers must have sensed Mikey's competitive personality from the many bike route maps he had drawn, because they concluded he would not have stopped at the stop sign.

"Mr. Quint was apparently trying to travel through a pre-planned course as fast as he could. As he approached the intersection he would have had good visibility to the north of the traffic he would be merging into. He would have also wanted to keep up his speed through the turn because he would be riding uphill as he traveled south." This is something my sister Clarissa, who also is a biker, said he would have done the first time she saw the scene.

Packer continued, "He most likely lost control of his bike while making his turn because of loose gravel or other debris on the roadway. The narrow, smooth touring tires on his new Trek could not handle corners on loose gravel as well as the wider, cleated tires on his older mountain bike. This difference may explain why he lost control this time, even though he had previously ridden his mountain bike through the same corner." This was exactly what my husband said the first time he saw the accident site.

Packer Engineering discussion:

> Based on all the information and analysis conducted to date, we believe the following scenario to be accurate: On June 15, 1993, Michael Quint was riding his new Trek 1200 bicycle on a 23.1 mile country road course. He had previously mapped, ridden, and logged his time over this route on May 8, 1993, with his mountain bike. He was probably riding his new touring bike fast, trying to beat his own record for that route. Two point six miles into his 23.1 mile route, riding downhill on Buck Lake Road, he approached the T-intersection of

County Road 200 West

With good visibility of the southbound traffic, he would merge with onto County Road 200 West. He made the decision to run through the stop sign and maintain good speed into his right turn. The more speed he could maintain in the turn, the easier he would be able to climb the hill on County Road 200 West. Near the middle of the turn, Mr. Quint lost control of his bike when his tires momentarily lost traction due to gravel, sand, or other debris on the road.

When the loss of traction occurs, a rider's normal instinct is to attempt to regain control of the bike. As the rider is regaining control, the bike does not travel in the intended turning radius, but rather generally travels straight from the point of lost traction. Mr. Quint apparently regained control of the bike, but not soon enough to stay on the southbound side of Country Road 200 West (or he had already crossed into the northbound side of Country Road 200 West). Once the danger was apparent, it appears that he attempted to avoid being hit by trying to ride completely across County Road 200 West in front of the northbound car. His front tire was approximately at the east edge of the road when the collision occurred.

By her own estimation, the driver was traveling about fifty-five mph as she approached the hill before the Buck Lake Road T-intersection. She had probably slowed down a little due to a lack of forward visibility as she crested the hill. She noticed a cyclist traveling fast down Buck Lake Road and may have started to apply her brakes prior to his losing control in the turn. When she realized that the cyclist was riding into her path, she steered toward her right, slamming on her brakes. This action locked her brakes, causing the car to continue moving in a straight line through the collision area. The car continued straight until the right side tires were on the grass, which caused the car to rotate counterclockwise due to the split friction coefficient. When the car was almost stopped, the driver released the brakes which made the car come back onto the road before coming to a stop.

My discussion:

He almost made it—almost. If he had had only a couple more seconds he could have made it to the other side of the

> road. Just a couple more seconds. If only the driver had not been going faster than the posted forty mph speed limit as she crested the hill, perhaps she would have arrived a few seconds later. Or if her brakes had not locked up she could have steered away from him instead of into the grass where he was heading to escape the impact. He only needed a few feet, a few seconds to live. Mikey tried his best to survive. He was not lucky that day. He ran into someone who was in a hurry. He paid with his life.

The more I thought of this accident, the more mind-boggling the timing seemed. It seemed like it was timed precisely to kill him. My mother had asked me, "Why did he have to die from it?"

You hear of many miracle accidents where people survive. I have even heard of bikers being hit by cars and surviving. Why was this accident timed so perfectly to kill him? I recalled that Mikey's neck was broken very high. Had he lived he likely would have been a quadriplegic; he would have hated it. I thought back to a passionate debate I had with the nurses in a sociology class I was taking a few months prior to Mikey's accident. I said I hoped a doctor would mercifully give the do not resuscitate order for me if I were to end up a quadriplegic. The nurses were insisting that life, even as a quadriplegic, was worthwhile. I said for me that would not be true. Mikey almost made it, but he did not. I wondered if there in the grassy ditch, his soul chose to not live as a quadriplegic. Although my husband and I would have happily devoted our lives to caring for him, I could honor what I know would have been his choice.

In retrospect, that debate about being a quadriplegic had the feel of another omen. At the time, of course, I didn't recognize it as such. I also recalled that my husband and I took a community course in CPR, getting our certificates on June 14, 1993, the day before his accident. We had never taken a course together previously or since. We never used our training. Was that another omen? And, there was still the matter of the premonitory dream I had ten months before the accident. Was it like the accident scenario? Yes, indeed it was. The fast ride down to a T-intersection. The cornfield ahead in the distance. The transparent rectangular monolith of deadly force on a collision course was the car windshield that killed him. The giant-sized radiator grill was his close-up view. The car tires that churned up the umber-colored soil next to the gray asphalt roadway at the collision point. The fatal outcome. But, the dream had confused me because it started with our taking a boat ride. I told Mikey about the dream and that I thought it might be the boat, so that exact scenario had not played out. The dream then shifted to a movie theater. Since the scene was shrouded, I was not able to see that he was coasting on a bicycle. The corn in the dream was also deceptive because it was high as it would be in August. It was newly planted in June. Nevertheless, it symbolized the hidden danger I sensed coming from the right. The dream stopped at the moment of collision, when the tires were churning up the soil, and when he would have been knocked unconscious. In the dream I felt what he was feeling and now know I was riding my bicycle at the same time. I take comfort that in the dream he was so happy. He was looking back at us and smiling. I can temper my guilt realizing that we were not in the movie scene with him as we were in the boat. That says to me that we could have done nothing. We were powerless to change his fate.

The many premonitions I had during those months prior to his death have tormented me for years. Even though most of them were vague and their language obscure, I was riddled with guilt. I judged myself as too stupid to understand the warnings. Of all of them, the dream tormented me the most, because the message was clear and I attempted to act on it. When my actions were to no avail, I didn't have the courage of my convictions. I ignored or didn't understand further warnings. I felt like an utter failure. Where did the dream come from? What was the purpose of the dream if not to prevent the accident? If the accident was meant to be, then it really wasn't an accident. There are some who say there are no accidents. Does this mean that our lives are pre-planned? Predetermined? Do we come into this life with a certain purpose and leave when it is completed? Mikey died clean and sober. Was that his purpose in this life? My niece Caroline told me she had a dream of Mikey about a month after the funeral. She said he was wearing his usual casual dark slacks and white shirt, and he had an Olympic-type medal around his neck. I immediately thought it was his reward for conquering alcoholism. Having met that challenge in this lifetime, was it truly his time to go? Do we live many lives as many religions have believed?

It is true that the reconstruction of the accident provided precise facts about what physically happened that day, but it left behind more questions unanswered—about fate, the meaning of dreams, and the nature of reality. Did Mikey hear a clarion call and leave work early that day to meet his fate? How could a mere dream foretell an accident? Is there another dimension where spirits of our ancestors watch over us and send us warnings of future events? Perhaps there is no past, present, or future, only one eternal time that can occasionally be glimpsed in a dream. If that is true, it is not possible to change anything. I could not grasp these ideas, nor did they ease the guilt I felt. For whatever reason, I must have known at some level what was going to happen, but I could not prevent it. That was my personal reality—the incomprehensible and inconsolable death of my beloved son in this world, at this time.

CHAPTER 16

Strange Happenings

Strange things happened around the house in those first months after Mikey died. Light bulbs kept burning out with quite a flash and sizzle. The telephone would often ring and no one would be there. Since there was no hang-up, it obviously was not a misdialed number. I never got that telephone company error recording, "If you want to make a call, hang up ...." Nor did I hear that siren-like signal that sounds when a phone is off the hook too long. In other words, the call was not originated on my end by some fluke. I could hold the line open for a long time and hear nothing. There was just dead silence. I can't remember that ever happening before. Now, it was happening repeatedly.

There was one time a person was actually on the line. A couple weeks before my birthday in August, an image of Mikey kept popping spontaneously into my mind. I saw him sitting at a desk, leaning forward with his arms folded. A telephone was the only object on the desk. He had a mischievous look on his face. I kept wondering why I was getting such a comical image in my mind. Then, on my birthday, at around 2:00 AM, the phone next to my bed rang. Half asleep, I picked up the phone and a man's voice in a southern drawl, said "Happy birthday, darlin'." I couldn't believe it.

I was amused and just said, "You have the wrong number." The caller apologized, embarrassed. I always felt that my son, the electrical engineer, somehow redirected that call to me to wish me a happy birthday.

The first Thanksgiving holiday was approaching. I was planning the usual meal with all the trimmings as I had for thirty-four years. Mikey loved "Turkey Day," so we were trying to celebrate it in his memory. After marinating my turkey with garlic and seasoned oil and making the bread stuffing, I was very tired and went to bed around midnight. A couple hours later something half awoke me from a dead sleep. I was very groggy. A few seconds later, the phone rang. It was that strange connection again. No one responded to my "Hellos." I hung up the phone and lay back on the bed, wondering if I had dreamed that the phone rang. However, both my husband and daughter heard the phone ring too and got up to see who was calling at such an odd hour. I believe it was Mikey calling. He never missed Thanksgiving. I wished I had not hung up the phone so quickly.

As fall drifted into winter, I spent evenings in the den, lying on the same couch where just a year ago I had reminisced about Mikey as a child. Now, the large picture that hung over the couch would make sharp crackling sounds as if the glass in the frame was breaking. I would get up to inspect it, but there were never any cracks in the glass. The picture never did that before. In fact, I never had any picture do that. As the nights grew longer and colder, the crackling sounds continued. I wondered if the cold outdoors was affecting the glass on the picture because of its metal frame. Yet, the windows in the room were not crackling; only the picture hanging over the couch was being disturbed by something.

During those early months Mike, Peggie, and I all had many dreams of Mikey in beautiful places. I saw him running through fields of lush tall grass with his dog, Spike, beside him. He was running on the other side of a winding creek toward his cottage that was next to the stream. There were mountains in the background enveloped in a rose lilac mist. In another dream I saw him standing next to a high waterfall in a forest of large pines. Mike saw him skiing down the slopes in Colorado. I met him once at the Grand Canyon. I saw his face. He had tears in his sad eyes. I awoke one morning and knew I had spent time with him in the beautiful world where he now lived. I felt such peace in my heart. Peggie had a powerful dream in which Mikey wanted to show her a magnificent sight. He took her hand and led her through the woods to a beautiful tree. High up in the branches was a white bird glowing with radiant light. She later drew a picture of that dream. Every year since then she searches for Christmas cards with a white dove to mail to friends and family at Christmastime. She called it the blessing bird.

Peggie's drawing of her dream of Mikey showing her the blessing bird

In spite of all our dreams, it seemed there was still no consolation for our grief. We were bravely trying to carry on, but we weren't doing very well at all. Sometimes for a split second when I first opened my eyes in the morning I would forget that Mikey had died; then I'd remember and a wave of nausea would overcome me. One day my mother took me aside and told me, "You'd better watch Mike." She was afraid he was going to kill himself. It is true that my husband and I each had thoughts of suicide and secretly devised foolproof plans to kill ourselves. I decided I would stand in front of the commuter train I used to take into Chicago to go to school. Mike was going to tie himself to his sailboat out in Lake Michigan and shoot himself in the head. How sad it was that we each wanted to use a vehicle that had once brought us joy to end our lives. Separately, we each decided that we could not heap even more misery on those we left behind, especially our daughter. Peggie also had thoughts of suicide. She turned to alcohol to deaden her pain because she knew her parents could not endure losing their other child. It isn't that we really wanted to stop living. We just wanted the excruciating pain to stop.

I realized I had never really *felt* death before Mikey died. I've known intellectually that everything dies. People die; pets die; I would die. I had been to many family funerals. My grandparents died. My father died. A good friend died. My cousin Leah died at the age of twelve. She and I were playmates and the same age. Death was sad and I cried, but I never felt such gut-wrenching torment as I did now. In the past, it was more shocking than anything else. One day someone was here and the next day gone. It was perplexing that someone could vanish so completely, but you carried on because there was nothing else you could do. I even remember explaining that I did not want to go to anyone's funeral because I wanted to remember the person as they were when they were alive. I went to Mikey's funeral because I didn't want to let him go. His death ripped our hearts out. There was not even a moment of relief as the days rolled into months. It was like being squeezed in the jaws of a huge iron vise, the jaws closed just tight enough so you couldn't wiggle free, but not so tight as to kill you. Grief was a constant agonizing torture. My husband's mother died when he was just ten years old. He *knew* the unending years of despair that lay ahead. I was just learning. Grief was like waiting, waiting for something to change, waiting for happiness to return, waiting for your loved one to come back. When my mother was in her eighties and confined to a wheelchair she often became depressed. She would say she was waiting to die. Grief was not like waiting to die. Grief was waiting for something that would never happen, something you knew would never happen, but waiting nevertheless. Grief was the most hopeless feeling I had ever known.

CHAPTER 17

The Compassionate Friends

We realized we needed help because we felt as if we were dying ourselves. Perhaps professional counseling was what we needed. Peggie worked for a large corporation which provided employee counseling services as a benefit. She was entitled to three free half-hour sessions which her family could also attend. We decided to go. At the first session, the counselor looked through the pictures of Mikey we brought as we talked about him. I remember mentioning that Mikey loved history and sadly he was history now. The counselor actually laughed because he mistakenly thought I was making a joke. He seemed uncomfortable that death was a problem that could not be resolved. At the second session, I attempted to bring up my dream that tormented me so much. The counselor quickly explained that the dream was something I fabricated out of my worries about my son. I found it strange that he didn't ask what was in the dream or what I thought about it. He didn't even allow me to vent my feelings about it. To him, it was either unimportant or loony. A young woman counseled us at the third session, which fell just before the July 4th holiday. It was exhausting to have to start all over again with a different person. She seemed impatient, as if she had something more important to do. When the session was over, she cheerily told us to enjoy our weekend as she showed us to the door. I couldn't believe she said that. It had only been two weeks since we had buried Mikey; we were not enjoying anything. This "counseling" was not only disappointing, it also downright painful. In time, I came to realize that grief counseling is a field that requires specialized training.

I soon learned about a support group for bereaved parents called "The Compassionate Friends." It was a self-help group made up of families who had experienced the death of a child at any age from any cause. Its stated purpose was "to aid in the positive resolution of grief and foster physical and emotional health of bereaved parents and their surviving children." It was a national nondenominational organization with local volunteer chapters. There was no cost to attend. It turned out to be priceless.

In August, 1993, Mike, Peggie, and I started attending a local chapter that was about an hour's drive from our home. I still remember those sad, quiet rides as we headed north through the old river towns just as the sun was sinking below the horizon. As time passed, the seasons began to change, then the leaves started to fall and next came the snow. In the dark of winter we came to know our way by the feel of the road as it gently curved along the winding Fox River. The meeting room was donated by a local business for use after hours. It was well-lit and warm. The conference-size tables were arranged in a large rectangle so we could all see each other. We took turns bringing refreshments. Each session started the same way; one-by-one each bereaved parent simply stated the child's name, age, and the way he or she died.

"My son's name is Michael James Quint. He was hit by a car while riding his bicycle. He was thirty-three."

"My son is Mike. He was … killed … on … his bicycle."

"My brother is Mikey. He was hit by a car … we were close … in age." We could then add anything else we wanted to say. Sometimes it was anger at the mistakes of others, sometimes anger at our own mistakes, sometimes anger at people who said stupid things, or at God who didn't save our child. Sometimes it was about memories that brought both smiles and tears. Sometimes it was about debilitating depression. My husband and daughter were never comfortable speaking in group settings. Now they couldn't speak without breaking down in tears. I could barely speak because my voice trembled too much. We had been shocked into silence. However, the meeting was a place where I felt I could express my feelings and the other people listened and understood. These people did not pull away at the mention of your dead child's name. Nor did they look perplexed if your grief was the loss of an "adult child." I found it was helpful to utter my pain out loud.

I will never forget the bereaved parents in our original circle. Their anguished faces, their slumped shoulders, their trembling voices reflected all that we felt. There was a divorced woman, a poet and artist, whose four-year-old son had been hit by a delivery truck in their own driveway. Her agony was palpable. There was an elderly woman whose thirty-eight-year-old grandson committed suicide. I remember feeling a flash of anger because I felt that he chose to die when my son wanted to live. There was a couple whose forty-two-year-old daughter and only child died in a plane crash. They looked shell-shocked as they leaned on each other. There was a couple whose thirteen-year-old son was the only one of three teenagers to die when a dune buggy overturned. This mother was desperately trying to help others as a way to heal her own pain while her husband was raging with anger at God and consequently left his church. There was a teenage boy who died of an asthma attack. His mother felt guilty that she had missed his last doctor's check-up. There was a father who created a Web site for his teenage son. His face was ravaged with sorrow as he asked us all to visit that site. There was a young couple whose infant was born with heart defects and lived only a few days in the hospital. There was a single mother whose baby died of SIDS. The father was a soldier who had not been present in their lives. She was now totally alone. Next to us was a couple whose twenty-year-old son died of "undetermined causes." They said his girlfriend still came to visit them. I thought how fortunate they were. As time went on, more grieving parents joined while others left the group. There seemed to be no shortage of bereaved parents in the world. We certainly were not alone in the enormity of our pain.

As I look back now, The Compassionate Friends was like an intensive care unit in a hospital. Intensive care is required to keep severely injured people from dying during the most critical period. The group kept us alive by listening and caring when the rest of the world had moved on. We learned that everyone has a right to grieve in his own way and for as long as it would take. We learned practical things, like ways to get through the holidays, birthdays, anniversaries, and other special days. We learned that siblings are often overlooked in grief because the focus is on the parents. We learned that the strain of grief will either tear a marriage apart or make it stronger. The same is true of friendships. With the help of "love gifts," the group published a wonderful newsletter each month with personal stories. Peggie's promise to her brother was published, as was the poem we had inscribed on Mikey's headstone. There came a time when being around such raw agony was too painful anymore; so like others before us, we too drifted away from the group meetings. However, we continued to get the newsletters for years and joined the group for special candle-lighting ceremonies during the holiday season.

A national organization, The Compassionate Friends holds a conference once a year in various cities across the country. We had never attended any conferences because they were too far away. However, the 23rd National Conference was being held in Rosemont, Illinois, in June of 2000. By that time, seven long years had passed since Mikey had died. We had survived the most horrendous years of grief. We had followed many paths to find solace. By that time we didn't feel an overwhelming need to attend. I think Mike and I decided to go mostly because it was practically in our own backyard, and we couldn't pass up the opportunity. Also, there was a certain symbolism, because Mikey's birthday was June 23rd. Peggie accompanied us as she always did. The three of us had stuck together through all the painful years. She was a very loyal person and loving daughter.

The conference was held in a large professional building. Free-standing display boards had been set up in the foyer for bereaved parents to hang pictures or writings of their child. Surrounding the banquet hall were many side rooms where nearly one hundred workshops on different topics were conducted throughout the weekend. I searched through the list of workshops hoping to find something about premonitions. One that looked somewhat promising was "After Death Communications." We attended and recorded the entire two-hour workshop. An After Death Communication, or ADC, is a spontaneous contact that your deceased child initiates with you. It is a firsthand experience that does not involve a psychic or medium. The workshop facilitators discussed their five-year research during which they collected over 3,500 firsthand accounts of ADCs from bereaved parents. They categorized twelve different types of ADCs, including sensing a presence, hearing a voice, feeling a touch, smelling an aroma, and visions. ADCs can occur while awake, during dreams, in the alpha state or twilight sleep, on the telephone, or during an out-of-body experience. The final category was "things that go bump in the night," such as lights or radios turning on or objects being moved. ADCs often happen around significant dates and can occur even ten, twenty, twenty-five, or thirty-five years later! The purpose of the ADC is to bring a needed message to the bereaved to offer comfort, reassurance, and hope.

After finishing their presentation, the facilitators opened the floor to questions. I asked if any of their accounts involved premonitions. The facilitator dropped that topic in a hasty, almost embarrassed manner. He mumbled that a premonition was an entirely different type of experience which was beyond the scope of the workshop. However, he did mumble an opinion that premonitions were basically a forewarning, so one could prepare for the emotional shock. He quickly moved on to the next person. Because I found his reaction strange and dismissive, I sank into myself, only half listening to the remainder of the workshop. For well over an hour the workshop attendees stood before the group and related their personal ADC experiences. I actually didn't remember any of these stories until I listened to my tape recording nearly a decade later. With trembling voices, and often on the verge of tears, these bereaved parents told stories that were very moving. Some of the ADCs were convincing, but, in my opinion, others could just as easily been seen as wishful thinking. An understandable clutching at straws. In all these tales I found one shining jewel. A Hispanic man from South Carolina told his incredible story:

> My sixteen-year-old daughter died unexpectedly three days after she was diagnosed with mononucleosis. We were told she would be going back to school on Monday. She had written a poem about a week before that she was planning to take to school that Monday. I hung the poem on the picture board out in the hallway here. The poem talks about a girl in a white lace dress running through a field of flowers and

butterflies, enjoying life. Enjoying life! Then a hand touches her and tells her it is time to go. She says, "I don't want to go. I want to stay!"

The voice replies, "It's okay. All of this will be here." The girl accepts that response and goes. I had a very hard time dealing with that poem. (He chokes back tears.) I am saying this as a preamble.

A couple of weeks after her death, an elderly relative in New York died. I telephoned my mother that I could not go to the funeral. I could not deal with it at that time. On the day of the funeral, my mother telephoned me back and said, "You are not going to believe this. Your cousin from Florida who you have not seen in forty years told me of a dream she had. In that dream she was looking out of the second-story window at a field of yellow flowers. In the field there was a girl in a white lace dress running and laughing and enjoying life. The girl ran toward the house. In the dream, your cousin ran downstairs and opened the door. The girl had almost black hair and hazel eyes. She came in and said, 'Tell them I am okay. I am happy.' Then she ran off."

My mother went on to say that the cousin was perturbed by the dream and decided to tell it to her friend, who had a sixteen-year-old daughter. But that girl was fine. When the cousin came to the funeral in New York she told her aunt about the dream who then said that she must tell my mother the story. My mother went bananas! She got a picture of my daughter and showed it to the cousin who had the dream. The cousin said, "That is the girl I saw!"

Being male, sometimes we need to really be hit between the eyes in order to believe. I now believe there is a life that exists afterward and our children do wait for us.

At the time I must have been paying attention more to the demeanor of the father who was obviously still shattered by grief than I was to the implication of his story. As I listened to the tape I recognized its unique significance. Virtually all the other stories had been various forms of ADCs. This story was different because it involved a premonition. The cousin's dream fit into the definition of an ADC, but the poem the girl wrote prior to her own death was a premonition. As I see it, the premonition is what made the later dream so believable to the bereaved father. Without the premonition poem, he would have had little basis to believe that the girl in his cousin's dream was actually his daughter. With the poem there was no doubt. It was the premonition—the very topic the workshop facilitator would not touch with a ten-foot pole—that made this story utterly convincing. I also now agree that we need to be hit between the eyes in order to believe in an afterlife and that we will, indeed, see our children again. However, I think this skepticism is to be expected in our culture. As our society has become more scientific, more materialistic, and more youth-oriented, we also have become more dismissive of intangible things. The American culture is said to be optimistic, but we still find it difficult to accept a concept as incredible as life after death.

CHAPTER 18

Spirituality

As I learned in the sociology course I took at Northern Illinois University, modern America is a death-denying culture. We publicly deal with death by avoiding the subject. Other cultures throughout history have recognized death as part of life and have established rituals and celebrations for staying connected to their dead. In Mexico, *Dia de los Muertos,* or Day of the Dead, is a three-day holiday to welcome back the spirits of loved ones who have died. It is a time of gift-giving and family reunions. Altars are built in their homes then filled with flowers, candles, and mementos. They bake special foods, including skull-shaped breads and sugar candy, for the festivities. Cemeteries come alive with mariachis serenading both the living and the dead as families enjoy picnics with the favorite foods of their dear departed. On All Soul's Day, there is a procession through town that includes bicycle-riding skeletons. In the Victorian era, death was celebrated with grandiose funerals, ornate grave monuments, and year-long mourning periods with prescribed clothing and etiquette. It is interesting that the Victorians were open about death, but talk about sex was taboo. Today it is the opposite. We are open about sex, but talk about death is taboo. *Grief is very lonely today in America.* Strangers prepare our loved ones for burial. People are uncomfortable and clumsy when speaking about the dead. Businesses allow only three days for mourning, and only for the death of an immediate family member. Our dead are segregated in cemeteries that have gradually migrated to the outskirts of towns. The cemetery where Mikey was buried required that headstones be flat and hidden from view. The rationale was to make it easier to mow the grass. We also were not allowed to plant any flowers for the same reason. From the roadway, the cemetery looked like a park or golf course. It was rare to see people there unless there is a burial in progress. A week after Mikey was buried, my husband, daughter, and I went to the cemetery and spread a blanket on the ground beside his grave so we could just sit there quietly with him. A groundskeeper came by and told us no picnics were allowed in the cemetery. When he saw we were not having a picnic, he left us in peace. Why not a picnic? What if a picnic gave us comfort? Why not set aside one day each year for cemetery picnics? In the long years that follow a funeral, there are few culturally-sanctioned rituals for remembering the dead. The Native Americans mark the first anniversary with a soul-releasing ceremony where they burn items of the deceased in a sacred fire. Four times a year, the Jewish say "Yizkor," a prayer for deceased loved ones, which I found very moving:

> In this silent hour, I remember my beloved Mike. I remember the days we lived together in happy family union and thy love and companionship were my delight and comfort. Though thou hast gone from me, thy image and thy soul abide with me. I think of thee with gratitude and bless thy memory. Though death hath taken thee from me, the bond that unites us cannot be broken.

Yet, most of us mourn on our own, in private, and in silence. Our dead must be very lonely, too.

In this cultural climate it was The Compassionate Friends that provided a place for the bereaved to gather together. They helped us survive the most difficult months. They validated our feelings and provided practical ways to handle people and situations. As indispensable and wonderful as this organization is, it had one flaw. There was no component of spirituality. I understand they believed this was necessary because they served people from all religious faiths. Yet, death, like birth, is a spiritual event—a sacred event. There needs to be a way to understand the death of a loved one in a spiritual way. Sometimes religious articles made their way into the newsletters, but always with the disclaimer that The Compassionate Friends was a nondenominational organization. However, group leaders did tend to be religious people, so there was a bias toward the dominant religions. I once briefly mentioned my premonition at our local group meeting as we each spoke in turn. I got a quick, disapproving glance from our group leader. At first I thought I imagined that silent rebuke, but then another person commented that he'd come closer to the Lord after the death of his brother. This time, the group leader nodded approvingly. I did not appreciate the implication that it was only acceptable to express conventional religious ideas.

The Compassionate Friends probably equated spirituality with religious belief as most people do. In my mind, those are not necessarily one and the same. I consider conventional religion a belief system one is basically born into. In fact, some religions won't even recognize converts as true members of their faith. Most religions discourage questioning of their tenets and praise faith as the higher virtue. I think this is one reason that science and religion have found it difficult to coexist. Science encourages questioning. Its goal is truth, which is always tentative until the scientific theory is either proven true or false. Religion asserts that truth was revealed at some point in the past and, therefore, is absolute. If something contradicts that revelation, then it is the religious belief that must be preserved. The sad thing about religion is that it should also be a quest for the truth. There is no other field that is solely interested in spirituality. Yet, instead of recognizing that there may be more to learn about the true nature of the spiritual realm, religion clings to outdated concepts, refusing to change. Evidently, this rigid stance is meant to give the illusion of certainty. Perhaps I demand too much of religion; I expected it to be perfect; I expected it to be about eternal truth, when it is basically only an imperfect human social institution. There are those who say religion, true or not, is necessary to force us to be good. Many go through the motions superficially to conform to societal expectations. Some say they believe because it is too lonely or too scary not to believe. Others find comfort in tradition. Maybe some honestly do believe or at least believe their own interpretation. Yet, many bereaved parents did not find the solace they expected from their religious faith. In their most desperate hours it often left them more bereft.

I cannot say that conventional religion left me more bereft, simply because I never turned to it to begin with. I had learned long ago that I would find no satisfying answers there. There are obvious reasons for my disenchantment, including religion's bloody history and abuse of power. I went to Sunday school at a Methodist Church as a child, then through catechism when I was twelve to become a member. For the most part, church was a pleasant experience, although I remember crying my eyes out when I first learned about the crucifixion of Jesus. Then I dried my tears and firmly rejected both the idea that this was a gift for me from a loving God and the guilt that went along with it. When I was in my twenties I read the Bible in its entirety to see if I was missing something. I read every single scriptural word; I have never forgotten the shocking cruelty and pettiness I found in those pages, particularly toward women and others deemed less than perfect. The "good news" was eternal life, but it was conditional. Only an exclusive group that fulfilled certain requirements would be "saved." There was something mean and self-serving about that. I was surprised to learn that Biblical figures foresaw events in dreams. In fact, the word "prophet" means someone who foretells the future. Yet, psychic ability was later decried as witchcraft and witches were burned at the stake. As premonitions came to be seen as evil, people kept such thoughts to themselves. The mortal fear surrounding premonitions remains in the collective unconscious and still haunts us today. I was not able to reconcile these failings with what religion claims to be—the word of God. So I set aside the book religion of my childhood to search for a different vision of spirituality. I adopted the Native American term *Waken Tonka*—the Great Mystery—which implies that there is much we do not know and may never know. It is a term that opens the imagination and inspires reverence for all of creation. I, indeed, had a great mystery before me—a premonition of death.

After I mentioned my dream of my son's death at The Compassionate Friends meeting, the woman whose son died of "undetermined causes" took me aside to talk with me. She said she had a photograph of her son that was taken shortly before he died which showed a ghostly haze around him. She brought it to show to me at the next meeting. She didn't let anyone else see her doing that. Another mother told me she had a dream before her baby girl was born that she was going to lose her. The child died of a common illness before she was two years old. She told me this privately after we stepped outside the building. I was heartened to learn I was not alone with my premonitions of death or with my suspicion that such talk was considered problematic. I concluded that grieving people did not share these experiences publicly for fear of ridicule or, even worse, for fear of having them discounted. However, premonitions felt deeply significant to me, and I wanted to understand them. I wanted to know where they came from and what they meant. I did not believe premonitions were tricks of the devil, fabrications of a worried mind, psychotic aberrations, or even just plain coincidences. I believed our premonitions were spiritual occurrences that might be a link to the true nature of the spiritual realm.

CHAPTER 19

Coping by Reading

I've always loved school because I love learning things, just about anything. I especially loved college, and over time became a "professional student," collecting several degrees and subsequently amassing a huge library. My way of coping with Mikey's death was to read, to search for answers and inspiration in books. My husband's way of coping was take long walks in nature, to do physical work, and to garden. While he created beautiful landscapes and cultivated vegetable gardens, I read everything I could find about grief, death, and the survival of consciousness. I poured over grief self-help books; I read memoirs written by bereaved parents; I attended a workshop for grief counselors offered by The American Academy of Bereavement entitled the *Many Faces of Grief.* I took an excellent college course titled *The Sociology of Death and Dying* at Northern Illinois University, where I learned about the cultural variations of dying and grieving. I did all this with one goal in mind: to understand those paranormal happenings around the time Mikey died.

One of the first books I picked up was the classic work *On Death and Dying* by Dr. Elisabeth Kubler-Ross. During the 1970s, she sought to educate the American medical profession about more humane ways of dealing with terminal patients. Through interviews with these patients she identified five stages of grief: Denial, Anger, Bargaining, Depression, and Acceptance. Psychologists have since copied these five stages to explain other kinds of losses, including the death of a loved one. I did not find that these stages described my grieving experience. Bereavement is not a terminal illness and should not be forced into that mold. There are similar elements, such as anger and depression, but I have always balked at the term acceptance or closure. At the "Many Faces of Grief" workshop I attended, I found that counselors defined mourning as the process of detaching from the dead and redirecting emotions to a suitable living object. They spoke of resolving grief as if it were a problem to be solved. Their term "complicated grief" further implied that when grief has lasted too long extra therapy was needed to fix it.

Society also has a low tolerance for grief that is lasting "too long." I think this is more a matter of other people being uncomfortable with the subject of death and preferring it would be forgotten as quickly as possible, or, at the very least, having you keep it to yourself. A very religious relative of mine gently told me that I should not be thinking about Mikey anymore because he was dead. Instead, she said I should take comfort in thinking about Jesus and God. That struck me as unnatural and illogical. Jesus died over two thousand years ago, and we are still thinking about him. Mikey had only been dead a couple months at that point. I could no more stop myself from thinking about Mikey after he died than I could stop myself from reminiscing about him those months before he died. One day some proselytizing ladies knocked on my door wanting to talk about their religion. I let them in because I needed some company. Although the story of Jesus was familiar to me since childhood, hearing it now made me start to cry. Maybe it was because Jesus was thirty-three when he died—the same age as Mikey. Maybe, for the first time, I realized Mary was a bereaved mother like me. Her anguish over the death of her son is never mentioned in the Bible, or in church, or ever. Instead, the most human of emotions is dismissed as unimportant, while a barbaric, cruel act of injustice is recast as a glorious symbol of God's love. When the church ladies asked why I was crying, I said my son had recently died. Pretending to be concerned about my privacy, they gathered up their religious tracts and hurriedly left. Perhaps, hiding behind religion is just another form of death denial.

I found one book that put forth a very different view of the mourning process. *Greeting the Angels* by Greg Mogenson focuses on what occurs in the imagination of the bereaved where the dead continue their existence in images, dreams, and fantasies. It claims that when we bury our dead, we begin a whole new way of relating to them. Our dead continue to demand our attention. They continue to influence our lives. All cultures across all time have been intensely interested in afterlife questions. Some questions are philosophical or religious such as heaven and hell, reincarnation, and immortality. Other questions grow out of personal experiences with premonitions, near-death experiences, or after-death communications. All these perspectives contribute to our cultural understanding of death. The most striking idea I found in this book suggests that *soul* is generated by the mourning process itself. "Deep inside the grief of the bereaved, the dead are at work making themselves into religion and culture, imagining themselves into soul."[1] Most people will agree that famous historical figures like Gandhi, Freud, and Plato continue to influence culture long after they are gone. This book assures us that "fame is not a criterion for soul-making."[2] Every loss contributes to the collective unconscious built up since the beginning of time. Through mourning our dead, we contribute to the universal soul.

I found that this exceptional book had a unique and refreshing perspective on mourning. It expressed what I was honestly feeling. Instead of admonishing us to let go of our dead, it encourages us to continue feeling their influence upon our lives and *to live in a manner that has redemptive influence on their souls as well.* I knew my son was physically gone, but he was not dead to me nor would he ever be. We do not detach from our dead; we carry them with us always. This is not unresolved grief; it is not abnormal grief. It is what grief has always been and should be—a sacred expression of love.

As I continued to read all the books I could find about death, I found an abundance of material about what happens after death. There didn't seem to be much written about unusual events happening in the months before death. As I dug through the many memoirs written by bereaved parents, I was hard-pressed to find any mention of premonitions. However, I did find one unusual book, *Five Cries of Grief*, that revealed such experiences with some detail. It was written by Irene and Merton Strommen, whose adult son was killed by a lightning strike. In many ways, his death resembled the way our Mikey died, in the sense that it provoked the same kinds of questions. Their son seemed to be called out to meet his fate on a jogging path on a sheltered side of a mountain. These parents questioned the timing that led their son to be at that exact point at that precise moment in order to be killed—as I had done with Mikey. They said their son had been memorizing Psalm 139 in the Bible the day he was killed. In that Psalm there is the idea that our days are numbered, even before we are born. They also wondered if their son had unconscious knowledge of his impending fate. Although the parents in this book personally said they had no sense of foreboding as we did, some of their friends reported premonitions that they associated with this young man's death. In his cry for understanding, the father questioned the meaning of these premonitions. He wondered if they were coming from the inhabitants of God's invisible realm who knew when a person's numbered days were ending.

After their son's funeral, a young relative had a realistic dream that included information about his death that was previously unknown to her. She was convinced she had met her cousin in her dream and found him to be alive and fine. Although the premonitions and dreams experienced by friends and family caused these bereaved parents to briefly search for answers, they decided these phenomena were beyond human comprehension and were best left as a mystery. In the end, they returned to their religious faith for answers seeming to find solace in that choice. Although I certainly do not fault those who choose faith, I regret to say I regard it as the easy way out. Doesn't the Bible admonish us to seek and you shall find? Knock and the door will open for you? If we never attempt to understand incomprehensible things, we will never add to the knowledge of the world.

I read all fifty-six questionnaires in Appendix II of the book, *The Death of an Adult Child* by Jeanne Blank.[3] The questionnaires were answered by the bereaved parents who participated in the author's study. Only once did I find a clear example of a premonition of death. A mother whose twenty-year-old son had been shot to death described an incident that happened when her son was a child. Mother and son had gone to a department store to have his picture taken. The mother recalled, "As the camera lens closed, the thought came to me that this child would be shot by a gun. Both of us had watched the camera lens as it closed."[4] At that moment, mother and son looked at each other. She said her son was paralyzed by fear; "It was as if both our souls knew at that moment what lay ahead."[5] It was striking that this premonition occurred years in advance of her son's death, suggesting that it was fate.

In the introduction to this book the author cautions us that questioning one's religious faith could destroy that faith, and in the end it would not make the bereaved parents feel better.[6] However, the author further concedes that it is a risk many bereaved parents may feel compelled to take. Again, I do not understand this worry about offending religious faith. Why should religion be protected from truth-seeking? What if the truth about the spiritual dimension is even more glorious than that presented by any religion? Isn't that worth trying to understand? A romantic might have said that we should not ask questions about the star-lit skies, lest we destroy the beauty along with the mystery. I believe that learning about the universe, the millions of spiral galaxies, the possible solar systems, the monstrous black holes, and the preponderance of invisible dark matter only contributes to the awe-inspiring majesty of the world we live in. There are physicists like Michio Kaku who proposes in his book *Hyperspace* that we live in a multi-dimensional reality. What if the spiritual realm is one of these other dimensions? What if it is a parallel universe? An alternate reality? In his book *Wholeness and the Implicate Order* David Bohm posits that we live in a universe of undivided wholeness, rather than one constructed of separate tiny building blocks of matter.[7] He describes an implicate, or enfolded order, and an explicate, or unfolded order. To explain these orders, he gives an example of the signal coming to your TV set as the implicate order, and the picture that displays on your TV screen as the explicate order.[8] He saw the universe in constant creative flux between those two orders of reality. Perhaps the spiritual realm is part of the hidden implicate order that is all around us.

Obviously, I was one of those parents who felt compelled to ask questions about incomprehensible things. What happens when we die? Do our individual souls continue to exist in another dimension? How is it possible to foresee one's death? It seemed that the key to these questions lay in understanding what a premonition is. I hoped I was capable of finding an answer that at least satisfied me.

CHAPTER 20

Synchronicity

One of the most intriguing science courses I took in college was quantum mechanics. It was a physics course that struck me as equally philosophical and scientific. I remember a remarkable paradox about the "non-local behavior" of particles. I may not remember all the details perfectly, but I believe the general idea is correct. It had to do with measuring the spin of a particle that had decayed or split into two separate halves. One half had to have the opposite spin of the other half, because spin is a conserved quantity. The remarkable thing was if you changed the spin of one half, the other half spontaneously changed its spin to obey that conservation law—even though there was no longer a physical connection between them. Philosophically, this said to me that things are connected in ways we don't understand, and once things are connected they are always connected. I extended this beautiful thought to the moment the universe itself was created. If everything in the universe was once condensed into an initial singularity before it exploded in the "Big Bang," then surely everything is still connected at the quantum level. I found comfort in the idea that we all are invisibly interconnected forever. It is a concept that reminds me of the Native Americans prayer, "*Mitakúye Oyasin*!" Its translated meaning is, "We are all related!" Native Americans include all of creation in this spiritual blessing.

At the same time that quantum mechanics weakened the belief that everything can be explained in terms of the physical link of cause and effect, further experiments shattered another basic assumption of science: the independent outside observer. Light has or seems to have a dual nature: it either shows up as a particle or as a wave, depending upon what the experimenter decides to look for. In other words, the experimenter's thoughts affect the outcome of the experiment. The experimenter cannot be separated from the experiment. Thoughts affect physical reality. Mind and matter are not separate. A similar idea in the field of psychology was introduced by Carl Jung in his concept of synchronicity. He wanted us to understand that the realms of psyche and matter are not separate, but form one unitary reality.[9] Basically, synchronicity is the concept that something that spontaneously occurs in your mind can be meaningfully linked with something that coincidentally occurs in the external world. While one event does not cause the other, nevertheless, they are linked by a personal meaning.

For example: I had been at a party where the hostess decided to show us a DVD entitled *What the Bleep Do We Know*. I wasn't able to stay long enough to watch the entire video since my ride home had arrived, but I found it intriguing and wished that I could have seen it completely. About a week later I got a package in the mail from Amazon.com. Although I frequently ordered books from them, I had not ordered anything in quite some time. I opened the box to find the DVD *What the Bleep Do We Know.* I did not order it, was not charged for it, and do not know why it came to me. My name was on the mailing label, but another person's name was on the packing slip. That person was unknown to me and lived in a town far away on the west coast. It was an error that I regarded as a synchronistic gift from the universe.

The telephone call I got on my first birthday after Mikey died was a synchronistic event. The mischievous image of Mikey sitting by a telephone kept popping spontaneously into my mind. Then I got a call on my birthday from an unknown man wishing me a happy birthday. What a wonderful birthday surprise!

A synchronistic event occurred around the time of my daughter's wedding. In October, 1995, the first planet outside the earth's solar system was found revolving around a star in the constellation Pegasus. I first heard that this solar system had two planets: one close to the star and one much further out. The man she married had two sons. My daughter became very close to the youngest son. The older son was always very distant from her. My daughter's nickname is Pegasus.

The dream of my son's accident was a synchronistic event. According to Jung, a synchronistic event can be foreseen in a dream and take place later in the external world.[10] Jung further explains that synchronistic events tend to occur around life's critical or stirring moments. When emotions are aroused, the unconscious mind becomes dominant, allowing something he called the "archetypes" to be constellated. Events, such as first love, weddings, birth, and death arouse recurring patterns of thought and emotion shared by all humanity. Jung proposed that synchronistic events always arise when an archetype is activated.[11] Physical science has long maintained the stance that we live in a meaningless universe created by chance. Synchronicity says otherwise. It connects things not physically, but purely through their meaning as perceived by the human observer.

Jung suspected that all forms of telepathy and precognition were based on the concept of synchronicity.[12] He hypothesized that a field of absolute knowledge permeated the totality of existence. This implied that at some higher level everything is already known. Different paths of thought were all pointing to this same conclusion. The quantum particle spin paradox implied that the particles were reacting to a higher level of information. Bohm saw our world as a projection from a higher dimension of undivided wholeness. Mystics speak of gathering information from the Akashic record, "The Book of Life," where all that has happened is written. Information comes to us from this omniscient background in such a way that our unconscious mind seems to know everything, but does not know anything precisely.[13]

A premonition, then, is a compelling but diffuse image that must be decoded because it lacks precise information. It is a synchronistic moment that lights up like a firefly in the cosmic cloud of knowing. At these moments we get a glimpse of what is on that eternal record.

Like the mother and son who saw his fate in the closing camera lens, my premonition was also a glimpse of what fate lay ahead for my dear son. Does that mean my efforts to warn him were useless? Fate is such an ancient concept in this modern world. It's hard to accept that our lives could be predetermined in a world where we exert so much control over our environment. We like to think our destiny is in our hands. As Americans, we claim that we can do or be anything if we just put our minds to it. Synchronicity breaks through this illusion and invites us to see our lives with a different understanding. It humbles us with the undeniable and haunting feeling that we are always in the presence of a great mystery.

I am left with the conclusion that the purpose of my premonitory dream was not to prevent the accident as I had thought. Instead, it served to warn me of this impending tragedy so that I might prepare myself for it. This knowledge broke through to my conscious mind, and then lay in my subconscious, directing my thoughts and actions. Recalling memories unexpectedly through daydreams of him, responding unquestioningly to his requests, giving him all of the gifts on his Christmas list that last year, repairing the black Mercedes to seemingly be ready for the funeral, all came about because my dream had warned me what was coming and was preparing me for this soul-shattering event. My taking a leave of absence in 1992 from my job and my husband's decision to sell the bakery in 1992 allowed us more time to visit our son during his last year on earth. The premonitions were a gift from the universe, from those caring souls in God's invisible realm who knew how much we loved him and how his death would devastate our lives. Nevertheless, we were still devastated. He was the hub of the wheel in our family, and we simply collapsed when he was gone. We didn't understand the meaning of these premonitions. We didn't know what was happening to us. In our materialistic society, we had been taught to dismiss such things as unreal. We were not taught to listen to our souls.

I have also concluded that the source of premonitions is a field of absolute knowledge that lies outside of time as we understand it. It is a place where everything already exists, a place where past, present, and future are all one. That place is harder for me to comprehend than the concept of elastic time in Einstein's general theory of relativity. It defies common sense and everyday experience.

We live in a space-time world where the future has not happened yet. I have not cooked dinner yet today, nor finished writing this book. We witness the passage of time in all things. Foreseeing the future seems like an astonishing thing. We believe precognition is possible only to those with the special gift of "sight"—a third eye or a sixth sense. Those who can foresee the future have existed since the beginning of history. The Oracle of Delphi was consulted by citizens in ancient Greece. Nostradamus in sixteenth century France predicted events five hundred years into the future. Today, we tend to regard paranormal events as unscientific nonsense, psychological delusions, or magic tricks—yet we remain fascinated by them. We do not dismiss them entirely. Just as we are drawn to watch lions in cages at the zoo, we invite fortune-tellers to parties as entertainment. We visit psychics at obscure places on the fringes of respectable neighborhoods for tarot card readings and horoscope castings. We are rightly suspicious that many may be scammers, but there are scammers in any line of work. Yet, I absolutely know that seeing the future is possible because of my own vivid dream of my son's fatal accident.

There are also those gifted people who can access unknown information from the ancient past. Many years ago I read about the remarkable life of the famous American clairvoyant Edgar Cayce, known as the "Sleeping Prophet," who died in 1945. He would fall into a self-induced hypnotic trance and give readings about medical conditions as his secretary recorded his words. Cayce had no memory of what he said during those readings. Once, when asked what happened during the trance, he described going out-of-body to a hall of records, somewhat like a library, for his information. Cayce described these records as written by each individual upon the skein of space and time. His description resonated with Jung's concept of the universal collective unconscious.

During one of Cayce's readings, he advised the person that his present medical affliction was the result of things that happened in several of his past lifetimes. When he awoke and was told that he had talked about past lives, confirming the existence of reincarnation, he was conflicted.[14] He was a devout orthodox Protestant inclined to believe that reincarnation was sacrilegious and contrary to the teachings of Christ. However, there are Biblical scholars who argue that references to reincarnation were removed from the Bible during the first century of Christianity. Others find passages still in the Bible that they interpret as indicative of reincarnation. In any case, the law of reincarnation continued to come up often during Cayce's readings. He revealed that our previous lifetimes continue to affect our current life both physically and psychologically. He believed that we come to each lifetime to learn soul lessons as we make our way to union with God. This may sound as if our lives are completely mapped out, but Cayce was careful to point out that we have free will. Free will is always stronger than destiny. We are able to make choices along the way. A soul may even choose a difficult life in order to gain some important life experience, but it is always the choice of the individual. This gave me a new perspective about people with difficult lives. Instead of feeling sorry for them, I saw them instead as courageous souls who decided on taking a hard course, an "honor's course," in the school of life. Yet, as I live this difficult circumstance as a mother whose son died tragically, I don't feel courageous. Even though I felt I earned a purple heart, it was because I was suffering a grievous wound. I don't understand what lesson I was supposed to learn. I didn't need to learn to love him or value him. I already did. I normally didn't need to be bludgeoned with a lesson. The meaning of this lesson, if there is one, escaped me. I had no idea what the lesson could be other than to learn to listen to my soul.

Whether reincarnation is true or not, it can be a practical philosophy, providing an eternal perspective to our lives. It certainly would guide us to live more moral lives if we knew we had to come back again and again to face the consequences of our actions until we were enlightened. One aspect of reincarnation I found especially comforting was that we often reincarnate with those we have lived with and loved in our previous lives. In her book, *Children's Past Lives*, Carol Bowman compiled stories about children who speak so innocently and knowingly about living before with the same people. It may have been a soul memory that inspired me to add the words, "Until we meet again," to Mikey's headstone.

I have come to believe that the premonitions my husband, my daughter, and I had of Mikey's impending death were a collection of images, sounds, smells, and feelings emanating from the field of absolute knowledge outside of time. They were synchronistic glimpses we were only able to see because of the enormous impact his death would have on our lives. Over the years, these premonitions had tormented me with guilt as I struggled to comprehend their purpose and source. I now realized that in focusing on and obsessing about them, I may have lost sight of the forest for the trees. If an eternal record exists, it implies a plan and a purpose to our lives. It implies a universe with spiritual meaning.

CHAPTER 21

The Psychomanteum

Many years ago, when I was in my midthirties, I read a book by Dr. Raymond Moody, Jr., MD, entitled *Life after Life*. I must have chosen that book to read because it was a very difficult period in my life. A good friend had died. Less than a year later my father died. Within a week of his funeral I was diagnosed with a rare benign tumor on my right jugular vein that had ruptured my right eardrum and wrapped around vital facial nerves. I went through four painful years of repeated surgeries that caused some facial paralysis and hearing loss before the tumor was eradicated. When Mikey died, I found I once again needed to read *Life after Life*. The book was unique in that it was a medical study rather than a religious proposal. Dr. Moody collected accounts from hospital patients who died on the operating table and then were resuscitated. These patients told him what happened when they died. Over and over again, he found a similar pattern of elements that included separating from the body, going through a tunnel toward a bright light, and being greeted by deceased relatives. The fact that there was a universal pattern seemed to prove that life continued after death. Dr. Moody coined the term "near-death experience," NDE, for this phenomenon. Since his groundbreaking work, new researchers have written numerous books on the subject documenting hundreds of accounts, including those of children. These accounts described leaving the body, viewing all the resuscitation efforts from above, and feeling no pain.[15] I read everything I could find on the subject because I had agonized about what Mikey felt when he was hit by that car and lay dying in the grassy ditch. All these wonderful stories greatly comforted me, and I was convinced that the near-death experience was genuine.

However, I also found that there were scientists who insisted that the near-death experience was an illusion caused by randomly firing synapses of the dying brain. I gave thought to this criticism. I reasoned that these same skeptical scientists undoubtedly believed in the theory of evolution. So, my question to them is: why would our brain evolve to create such an illusion? It is only with the recent advances of medical science that we have been able to resuscitate people who have died; so in my mind there could have been no evolutionary advantage to such an illusion. If we just die, why not simply fade to black? Who would know? Scientists have also shown that there is an area in the brain that can be electrically stimulated to produce elements of a near-death experience, thereby concluding it can't be "real." Then it also cannot be a random firing of synapses if there is a specific area in the brain devoted to it. So, I still propose the same question. Why would our brain have evolved a specific area in the brain just to create a pointless illusion? I reasoned instead that this area in the brain could possibly be a doorway to the next dimension.

Dr. Moody and other researchers found that near-death experiences profoundly and positively affected the people who had them. In particular, they lost their fear of death and realized what was truly important in life. Probably the most healing aspect of the near-death experience was meeting deceased relatives. Dr. Moody decided to expand his research to find a way to recreate this element of the near-death experience. Coincidentally, the same year Mikey died, the results of this research were published in his book, entitled *Reunions: Visionary Encounters with Departed Loved Ones.* In this book he described a way to deliberately evoke apparitions of the deceased in a controlled setting. The purpose was to facilitate a reunion with loved ones lost to death in order to bring consolation and solace to the bereaved.

The proposed method involved gazing in the mirror, which he believed could open a doorway to what he called the Middle Realm, a mysterious region of the unconscious mind where the living and dead could meet. He immediately found that this research was not as well-received as the near-death studies because of the occult stigma associated with mirror gazing. In reviewing the long history of mirror gazing, he found that it had been suppressed or ignored for several reasons. He points to the fear of what might come up from the unconscious, religious claims that it is demonic, scientific claims that it is hallucinatory, and the impatience of the modern world that cannot slow down enough to experience an altered state of consciousness. However, spontaneous visions of the deceased have been recorded throughout history. Dr. Moody retold a remarkable story of General Patton who had a vision of his ancestors watching over him on the battlefield. He related a well-known story of President Abraham Lincoln who saw a ghostly image of himself in his coffin just prior to his assassination. He also discovered cultures where evocation of the dead played an important role. In ancient Greece, apparitions of the dead were purposely evoked at places called Oracles of the Dead, or Psychomanteums. One of these sites was excavated in Greece in the 1950s. The excavation revealed an underground maze of tunnels that led to an apparition chamber where an enormous, polished bronze cauldron would have been filled with a liquid. Seekers prepared for the experience through a long process of sensory deprivation by remaining in the dark underground for up to a month. After this time, they would enter the apparition chamber and gaze upon the reflective surface of the liquid in the cauldron to see their visions. In essence, this was a spiritual retreat with the purpose of consulting with one's ancestors.

To put mirror gazing to the test, Dr. Moody built a modern-day psychomanteum, which he called the Theater of the Mind. My husband, my sister Carole, and I attended a workshop there in April, 1994, to learn his technique. The Theater of the Mind was located in an old gristmill next to a bubbling creek in a secluded wooded setting in rural Alabama. The décor inside the gristmill was designed to alter the sense of time and predictability. There was mind-bending art work, a paranormal library, and odd mishmash of antiques. There were no clocks in sight—only an ancient sundial.

The apparition chamber was in a small, attic room on the second floor of the gristmill. In the room was a four-foot-tall mirror which was about three feet above the floor. An old-fashioned, high-backed, easy chair with dark upholstery was positioned about three feet in front of the mirror. The back legs of the chair had been shortened in order to position the viewer at the proper tilt so he could not see himself in the mirror. The room was dimly lit by a nightlight placed behind the chair. Preparation to establish the proper frame of mind before entering the psychomanteum lasted nearly all day. It included walks to enjoy the beauty of nature and reminiscing with Dr. Moody about the loved one you wished to see. Dr. Moody was a very unassuming personality for all his renown. He was thoughtful and approachable. I could see how his demeanor would relax his clients completely before they entered the apparition chamber to gaze in the mirror. Dr. Moody facilitated the many reunions he had described in his book in this same manner. He then personally told us of the remarkable reunion he himself had with his grandmother in the psychomanteum. It was amusing because the "wrong" grandmother showed up. It was healing because it was actually the grandmother he needed to mend fences with. He said that his "reunion" was just as real as an experience with any human being—as real as his sitting there talking to us. His first-hand account totally convinced me it was truly possible.

Since there were a large number of students at the workshop, there was not enough time for each of us, or any of us, to try out the apparition chamber. Most participants were professionals in the field of grief therapy who had come to learn about this new tool. One woman was a hospice chaplain and later wrote her own book about after-life encounters. A well-known man who investigated paranormal phenomena also gave a talk to the group. The most memorable, to me personally, was a woman from New York whose specialty was the grief at the loss of a companion animal. My husband and I sat and talked to her privately. She was willing to listen to my premonition dream in complete detail. She asked if I had told anyone about it before it came true. My husband confirmed that I had told him about it months before it came true. She did not dismiss my premonition, rather she simply said, "So, you knew." I told her I felt like I was being punished. She seemed dismayed and gently reminded me, "Death is not a punishment." Her counsel was very comforting and reassuring, but she lived too far away for us to see her again. I remember two men who were into Native American spirituality. I especially remember a businessman named Mike who initially annoyed me to distraction. He kept getting up and down during discussions to reposition himself or to temporarily leave the group. I usually ended up with his large rear end in my face as he struggled past me. He suddenly appeared once again in my face on the last day when we were taking pictures of various attendees. So, I snapped a picture of him. When I developed the picture, there was a ghostly apparition around his head. I got his address and mailed it to him. He was thrilled because he thought it was his dead father. I thought it was Mikey. We each thought it was the person who we were trying to reach. I have learned since, that if something is annoying you, something is "in your face," often it is a sign that a significant lesson is about to happen.

The workshop lasted two days, after which we received a Theater of the Mind certificate in Psychomanteum Facilitation. In other words, we were now qualified to run a psychomanteum. I did not think that one could achieve what Dr. Moody had taken years to perfect in two days of training. However, I enjoyed being there and meeting Dr. Moody. He signed my copy of his book:

> Dear Jane,
>
> It's been delightful to get to know you.
> Please keep in touch if we can help in any way.
> I lost a son, too, so I understand how hard it is.
>
> Love,
>
> Raymond

CHAPTER 22

Far Journeys

After returning home from the Theater of the Mind workshop, I was anxious to get into a psychomanteum to have a reunion with Mikey. There was a person at the workshop who ran a psychomanteum at his home in Florida. He was quite adamant that he had outstanding success and privately boasted that it was far better than that of Dr. Moody. My sister Carole and I flew to his home in Florida and were surprised to find it was in a trailer park. The apparition chamber in his trailer was small and cozy, and we took turns going in and out for short periods of time. Between sittings we were shown some unusual items. One was some type of small glass ball in which different animals seemed to appear as you gazed at it. I imagined I saw bears, which I was then told were a sign of courage. Another was a book on the paranormal that had pictures of four-inch spheres floating in the air that were purported to be spirits. I became suspicious when I went back in the psychomanteum and saw those exact spheres floating there. When I came out I was immediately asked if I saw any "spirits." I felt I was being manipulated, so I said "no" out of spite. Besides, I just couldn't accept that the four-inch sphere was Mikey! I suspected that there was some type of hologram equipment creating the illusion. The man's look of disbelief that I didn't see spirits confirmed my suspicions. He told us interesting stories while we ate a simple meal his wife had prepared. He told us that when he was a child in the South, he knew an old, black man who saw visions in the water of a deep well. He told me my aura was deep blue, meaning I was a teacher. I was astonished to learn that another person in the trailer park also had psychomanteum! Although he certainly wanted our experience to be a success, he was an opinionated, retired military man with whom I did not resonate well because of his domineering personality. That may have been the reason I did not have a visitation. It also may have been that I did not trust that what was happening was genuine. The experience had the feel of a gimmicky magic show. All I remember of the lunch was a whipped-cream pie made with packaged instant butterscotch pudding that later left a bad taste in my mouth. As we left we were cheerfully told, "Y'all come back now, y'hear!" We laughed as we drove away from the trailer park in our rented car.

I soon received a professional-looking brochure in the mail for a psychomanteum in Arizona run by two women who had taken Dr. Moody's training. I made an appointment, and Mike, Peggie and I drove the fifteen-hundred-mile trip there by car through the autumn heartland. We reached a beautiful, sprawling adobe-style house located in the spiritual vortex area of Arizona. The landscaping was typical for the Southwest, with cactus plants and a pebble lawn. As we were the only clients, the entire day was devoted to us. We sank into deep, comfortable, white-leather sectional couches in the living room where we talked about Mikey with the facilitators. We were a little impatient with the talking. We wanted to experience the psychomanteum! The facilitators kept the pace slow, serving a light lunch of zucchini salad and fresh fruit out on the patio. We were thrilled to see hummingbirds hovering around huge, drooping angel trumpet flowers. On the way to Arizona we had decided if we saw a hummingbird at the home, it would be a sign that Mikey was there with us. Having our sign, we were hopeful as we each took our turns in the apparition chamber located in a spare bedroom of the home. It was equipped with a special oscillating chair to help induce an altered state of consciousness, as well as headphones for listening to ethereal music. There was a large mirror on the wall. I was the last one to go in the psychomanteum, and I was in there a very long time—at least an hour, perhaps two—when the mirror finally started to cloud up with a gray mist. Right at that moment, the facilitators barged in the room! I was so upset! I felt something was about to happen and they had ruined it! We were not allowed to see each other as we took turns, so I didn't find out until later that Mike and Peggie also had no luck. The facilitators tried so hard to relax us, but we just really couldn't relax. We were going to see Mikey any minute, how could we relax? They had followed Dr. Moody's method. There was no trickery involved. It just didn't work for us. We had made a far journey to no avail once again. However, there was one significant occurrence on our road trip to Arizona. Peggie woke up one night in her motel room and said that she saw a display of brightly colored whirling dots of light in the mirror over the dresser. In the parking lot the next morning, we saw a delivery truck with the name Angola, Indiana, on the side. What were the odds of seeing a truck from the little town where Mikey had lived? Synchronicity way out there in Arizona!

I decided to build my own psychomanteum in our home in Naperville. It was a very old home with thick plaster walls that completely muffled the sounds from the outside world. I converted my office into an apparition chamber. It was the same office where I received that horrible call that Mikey had died more than a year before. I made a thick, light-blocking panel for the windows, hung black velvet drapes, and laid a new black carpet on the floor. I purchased an expensive oscillating chair like the one in the Arizona psychomanteum and had it shipped from a company in California. My husband helped me make room-divider screens that I covered with black felt. I used the screens to create a small enclosure around the chair for a more cradled feeling. I bought a tape player with headphones for music. I often sat in my psychomanteum and tried to meditate. Yet, in spite of my countless attempts I was never able to have a reunion with Mikey. I did get to the point where I would occasionally see a beautiful geometric pattern of deep blue lights which I still see spontaneously at times to this day. After nearly a year, I concluded that I was too distraught, too anxious, and trying too hard. My mind was shattered in a million pieces when Mikey died. I likened it to a large pane of glass that had been slammed down on a concrete surface. I could not put the pieces back together. I could not recover from the trauma of losing him. I could not relax. I could not quiet my soul. Anything that might happen would only happen spontaneously when my conscious mind was occupied elsewhere. I dismantled my psychomanteum and turned in another direction.

CHAPTER 23

The Psychic Medium

I don't know why I turned on the TV just at that time that evening. It was only a month after Mikey died, and I had not been watching much TV. Remarkably, this program was about a man who claimed to communicate with the dead. I watched a nondescript man making random circling scratches with a pencil on a notepad on his lap as he gave a reading to an older, bereaved couple sitting across from him. He was able to tell them details that convinced them he was really communicating with their deceased child. I was astonished that such a thing was possible. This man's name was George Anderson. I came to find out he is what is called a medium. After watching the program, I ran out and got the book entitled *We Don't Die: George Anderson's Conversations with the Other Side* by Joel Martin and Patricia Romanowski. It described his communications with those who have died; it was totally convincing. Scientists from top universities rigorously tested his abilities and verified that something usual was occurring during his readings. In fact, he was the first medium to agree to such testing. Respected people such as Elisabeth Kubler-Ross believed that he was genuine. He was the first medium to receive approval for his own network primetime television specials, *Talking to the Dead*. In contrast to those spooky séances shown in ghost movies, George Anderson gave readings in a lighted room with no props—other than a scratch pad and pencil. It was up to the people who received the reading to determine whether or not they felt it had been a real communication. I could see the joy on faces of that bereaved couple. I could imagine feeling that same joy if I could speak to Mikey once again.

I was frantic to get a reading with George Anderson. However, he only set aside one hour on the first Tuesday of each month for accepting telephone calls to make appointments. As determined as I was, I could never get a call through. Meanwhile, George Anderson seemed to be appearing everywhere, on national television talk shows, in newspapers, and magazines. I wrote for information and found out that he also did personal readings, but only in Long Island, New York. A reading cost $1,200 for an hour session with one or two people. As desperate as bereaved parents are, not many could afford that fee, plus the cost of travel and hotel accommodations. However, he also did readings over the telephone, which made it only slightly more affordable. I put my name on a waiting list for a telephone reading, but I never got a call. I later learned that George was traveling to various large cities across the country doing personal readings. I hoped he would come to a city within driving distance of us one day, but I didn't have much hope of that happening. He was the most famous of the mediums and his organization reached across the globe. There were just too many bereaved people in this world.

Since I could not make contact with George Anderson, I searched for other psychics and mediums. I tried contacting the Edgar Cayce Foundation in Virginia Beach for such a recommendation. They were unable to give me any name. I searched out New Age book stores and magazines. There seemed to be an underground psychic network, but it was difficult to figure out how to hook into it. Most psychics had a specialty. Some gleaned information from personal objects; some from using tarot cards, through automatic writings, or by reading auras. Some predicted earthquakes or hurricanes. There were channelers and astrologers, love psychics and lottery psychics. The most fascinating to me were the psychic detectives who would help police solve missing person or murder cases. Many of those appeared on TV detective programs, which I watched avidly. However, I was unable to find a psychic or medium who communicated with the dead until I went to Dr. Moody's Theater of the Mind workshop. One of the facilitators there who helped with the training gave me the name of a woman who specialized in what she called "spirit communications." We had our first appointment with her on October 28, 1994, in Ohio. Since she had asked us to bring pictures, I brought photos of Mikey doing various things. She prayed over these pictures before meeting us in a small living room. The room was softly lit. We sat on comfortable couches arranged in a semicircle, facing her. We linked hands as she bowed her head and prayed. The session lasted nearly an hour, and she recorded it for us.

Although we certainly felt deep comfort after this spirit communication, I later wondered if the photos gave too many clues. There were things that came up in the reading that related exactly to the scenes in the pictures, but weren't really important to us. I realized that bereaved people are so desperate to contact their loved one that they might ignore such suspicions. Also, there was much in that session and subsequent sessions that I felt was instruction or health advice. She told us how she came to have her gift after a serious, incurable illness and how it helped her heal. She described the different levels of heaven which no one can prove or disprove. She also explained how reincarnation works, that only a piece of the soul returns to earth and that Mikey will be there to greet us when we die. She described in detail how reincarnation occurred in her own family. She also told us how we could learn to communicate ourselves by using a technique called automatic writing. Although we felt serene after this reading, I never felt a need to listen to the tape recording of that session after that day. We missed Mikey's physical presence. We missed talking to him directly.

Fifteen years later, in the process of writing this story, I decided to listen to the tape recording of that session. I was stunned. I think my mind must have been too shattered at the time to fully appreciate how amazing and potentially healing this reading was. Keep in mind that this psychic knew little about us before we sat down with her that day. In the next chapter, I will share portions of that session that I felt were genuine spirit communications—none of this information made me wary. It may have been my nagging suspicions that caused me to focus on the unremarkable parts of the reading. The truth is that there was incredible information that could not have come from photos, guesses, or any place other than the spirit world. Most important was the information about a premonition. Given my torment over my premonitions, I have no idea how I did not recognize the full significance of that revelation until now. Perhaps I was not ready to be relieved of my guilt.

CHAPTER 24

Spirit Communication

October 28, 1994—
Spirit Communication with Mikey

Psychic: To start, I would like each of you to give your full name and your age. Then give me the full name of your son and the day, month, and year he passed.

> *I gave my age as 55 and Mike gave his age as 58. At first, Peggie gave her name as Peggie, but then corrected it to her legal name, Margaret. She had just turned 34.*

Jane: Michael James Quint, he died June 15, 1993, on a Tuesday afternoon.

Psychic: You said your name is Margaret *(to Peggie)*. Is there a Margaret in the other world? An older woman? Is it your mother *(looking at Mike)*? Your mother is holding him. She is saying, "Tell them that I carried him home." There is a man also with her. This is a short man. Is this Grandpa?

There is a baby. They are picking up a baby and showing it to me. She is saying, "Would you tell Jane we don't lose them." I believe this is a child that didn't get to live. It could have been miscarried. It could have been aborted. Or it just had a very short life in this earth. Did your mother lose a child? Because she is picking it up like it is hers.

Mike: Some died shortly after birth.

Psychic: I need to get into his vibrations. When I move to them, I try not to disturb what is going on over there. When I do this it is like mental telepathy. He isn't speaking to me. I have to work it off them. If he says something and I don't pick it up, it is because of me, not because he isn't trying to tell me something. I work with energy or the emotions of him. I started to feel like I am filling up with water or blood and when this started to happen … I don't know if it is him or if it is Margaret, because they are touching right now.

> *Mike's mother, Margaret, died of drowning. Mikey suffered internal bleeding.*

Psychic: Did you know he had a dream; he had a premonition about something, a couple weeks before he passed? Do you know what he is talking about?

Peggie: He didn't tell us anything.

Mike: He was living away from home so we didn't talk too often.

Psychic: You have been with your son; he is talking about your visiting him in his world. He is saying, "You have been helping me, Mom." You have been over there taking care of him. Tell her that she has been with me. I have not had to do this all myself. Can you remember visiting with him? You have been going into the other world with him.

What happens is that you go out-of-body when you are in the delta or theta sleep. Your spirit is leaving. It can go into this other world. You may find yourself getting very tired. Take B12 shots to keep your energy level going. It is so magnificent in that world. It is like our world, only more magnificent. If you remembered it, you would want to die to go there. You have eternal life. God prepared a place for you. To be able to see this world I connect to the universal mind of God; I meditate working with God's energy. We are vibrations. You need to meditate to go slower and slower in order to see the other world, in order to speak with your son.

He says he is walking with you *(to Mike)*. What does he mean?

Mike: I go walking every day in the park. If I don't walk then I don't feel good.

Psychic: Well, he says he is walking with you.

Mike: Thank you.

Psychic: You can talk to him while you walk. Just acknowledge him.

Mike: I do.

Psychic: Peggie, he is talking about how loyal and how wonderful you are. He is opening his arms. He says he loves you so very much. He is taking flowers, he keeps laying out flowers in a garden, he is handing everyone a rose. He is giving you back flowers. I think you may have given him one. Are there flowers you may have given him, at his funeral? On his coffin? He is trying to say how much he appreciates it.

Have you noticed light bulbs burning out? They like to use the electrical system to get your attention. They also love to use the phone system. It's their way of saying, "Hello."

They also show themselves on pictures, especially on Polaroid pictures.

Jane: Yes, we certainly have noticed that. I even got a call on Thanksgiving, but no one was on the line.

Mike: And she hangs up! *(laughter)*

Psychic: He doesn't want you grieving and hating God. It wasn't anyone's fault. No one could have done anything. Were you feeling like you should have been able to do something? He is saying no one could have done anything. He may have had a premonition that it was going to happen. Did he mention a dream? He keeps talking about a premonition. He wants to talk about this dream.

Jane: I had a dream. (*I briefly told her about my premonitory dream of the accident.*) I tried to warn him, but he said I was worrying too much. He didn't want to hear it. As it turned out, my premonition was like it happened. I feel so guilty, because I failed to warn him.

Psychic: So, you had a dream that it would happen. *(pause)* Well, I thought that would stop him, but it didn't. He is saying he had a premonition.

Jane: I wondered if he had a premonition. He called me two weeks before he died and asked me to bring some bricks for his garden. When I asked him how soon he needed them, he said, "Pretty quick." I shuddered when he said that.

> *As I listened to this tape, I recalled all the times I felt he may have had a premonition. When I was at his house the day that I brought the yellow bricks, he seemed so much at peace as he showed me his flowers and played music for me on his new stereo. Even on the sailboat at the graduation party, I had the feeling he was looking at the landscape of the dunes like he was seeing it for the last time. Even as we kissed and said goodbye that last day, he seemed so sad. What I felt was true.*

Psychic: He keeps bringing up this dream. He wants to talk about this dream. It's not your dream. He said he had a dream. It was about two or three weeks before he passed. He said in his dream he was running. He said he was in a tunnel. He could see a light at the end of the tunnel. He knew if he could get to the light he would get out of the tunnel. I think first he was outside. He was in the mountains in Colorado, hiking. As he was exploring he found an entrance to a cave. He went inside the cave but he got lost. Then he felt like he was falling and falling. When he got on his feet he thought he had to get to the end of tunnel. He was running and running, trying to get out. Then he felt someone pushing him from behind. Someone was pushing him very hard toward the light. He said, "Push harder! Push harder!" He tried to look back at who was pushing him, but he couldn't see who it was. He said, "Then I woke up. I was sweating, my heart was pounding, and I said to myself, I am going to die."

You didn't know there was a premonition to his passing? He told someone. Was it his wife?

As I listened to the tape, I suddenly remembered something that happened the first days we were with Cristal in Angola—those first days when things were still good between us. I walked into the living room where she was talking to Mike. She was agitated and was talking about Mikey waking up one night from a horrifying dream. She said he was all wet with sweat. He got up out of bed all agitated. I don't remember her actually saying that he thought he was going to die, but she may have said that. I may have blocked it out, or she may have said it to Mike before I walked in the room. Remembering that scene from so long ago once again made me cry. I wished I could reach out and hold him and cry with him. Why didn't he tell me? Why? I was so afraid to talk to him about my dream again because I thought I was upsetting him. Knowing him, he probably didn't want to worry me with his dream. His dream didn't give him precise information, either. A cave and a tunnel? How was that a warning for a bike and a car? The dream got the message across that he was going to die without giving any information on how to prevent it. Oh, my God! He knew. We all knew and could do nothing. I cried, realizing he knew and spared us.

I thought of his dream, and I wondered how I would react if I had a similar dream about my own death. Would I be so at peace as he was? Would I be so resigned? After all, he was not ill. He did not have a disease. He was at his prime, in perfect health, had conquered alcoholism, was doing extremely well on his job, had just bought a new house and was starting out to raise a family. Why should he die just then? Would I be so at peace like he seemed to be? So gentle with others? What a brave soul he was to face that knowledge with such quiet courage. What a beautiful soul.

Psychic: He said that when he died he tried to get back into his body, but his body wouldn't take him. He felt like he was in his dream again. He could remember falling and falling. He thought he was still dreaming. His spirit was falling and falling, but he couldn't get up. He said, "I kept trying to stay alive, but I couldn't." All of a sudden it was like his dream, because he was running again. This time when he turned around, he saw who was pushing him. He said, "I know you. You are my guardian angel."

The guardian angel said, "I am here to help you."

> *I realized for the first time as I listened to the tape that Mikey's dream was not a dream about a fatal accident as my dream was; rather it was a dream about what happens at the moment of death. His falling into a tunnel, running toward a light, and being helped by a guardian angel sounded similar to the descriptions of near-death experiences. I was a true believer now. This is what my dear child was going through as he lay dying.*

Mikey protested to his guardian angel, "But I didn't say goodbye, I have to go back!" He could hear us screaming and crying for him. His guardian angel said he couldn't go back. Then he thought he was still in a dream. He thought he was still alive in the earth.

> *I remembered the apparition I thought I saw in his office; I remembered that Cristal said she heard him breathing in the bed next to her during the weeks after he died. I remembered she said the lights flickered at their place of employment when she went back to work after the funeral. That is when I thought he didn't know he was dead, and I started praying for his soul. I prayed and prayed for him to find peace.*

Psychic: When they go over there they go though the book of life as they are detaching from earthly things. The pictures are starting to come. He is showing me that he was not aware this was going to happen. He did not get to complete what he needed to complete. He said when he looked in the book of life he saw how hard your life was as a young boy, Dad. You never had anyone to love you or help you. That was very hard. We were given everything, but you didn't have it as easy. You gave us everything. We had the best of all worlds.

Mike: It was my pleasure.

Psychic: Margaret came to take him after he read the book of life. She embraced him and held him. They had been waiting for him. They had been told he was coming. I have a feeling that it was something that was going to happen.

Has his wife started to go with someone? That is what he wanted. He needed someone for her.

Jane: We don't know. We don't hear from her anymore.

Psychic: Are you planning to have any children? *(to Peggie)* What is the name of your husband? Not married yet? He's your boyfriend? What is your boyfriend's name? Have you two been talking about this? Oh, it's private … your parents are here! *(laughter)*

I wouldn't try to embarrass you. I am mentioning this because your brother picked up a baby. When he turned the baby toward me it had his face. When they do that, it means reincarnation. How it works is that your soul goes to God, but a piece of the soul can come back into the earthly body. That piece of soul is just part of that personality. He wants to come back into the family. If it happens—if you become pregnant—it will be him. Your body, your cells run too fast. It may keep you from getting pregnant. Your energy runs too fast. You may need to learn about self-hypnosis in order to relax. He wants to come back—but you don't have to have a child because of that. You don't have to get pregnant, but your biological clock is running out. He can come back to someone else in the family.

Peggie: I want him to come to me.

> *When we left this wonderful session in 1994, we were overwhelmed. It was so surprising that my husband's mother Margaret was the first spirit to come up. We didn't expect that in any way. She had been dead for nearly forty years. She had committed suicide by throwing herself in the Inn River in Austria when Mike was only ten years old. She had taken him for a haircut in town and when he came out she was gone … forever. A body was recovered, but they were never sure if it was her. The Catholic Church in St. Florien, where she had cleaned and ironed for years, would not allow the body to be buried in their cemetery because of her suicide. So, Mike had no grave to visit. He and his younger sister were placed in an orphanage, where they remained for about a year until his father remarried. When I met my husband, and during the early years of our marriage, I could not mention his mother without bringing tears to his eyes. He carried a picture of her in his wallet. He was still grieving. He hadn't recovered from the trauma. In those days, during the difficult years following World War II, no one paid much attention to helping a grieving child. He said his mother's appearance in this session was powerful and healing for him. But, that sorrow had already been eclipsed by the even greater sorrow of the death of his son.*

Although it took me fifteen years to realize it, the most healing aspect for me was my son's telling me about his premonition. No one in that room that day knew about his premonition. The dream with all its details could only have come from Mikey himself. I found his insistence in telling me his dream remarkable. The psychic could have let it go, but he was persistent in getting his message through. He knew how important it was that I know. He knew how guilty I felt because I tried to warn him and couldn't save his life. Still, it makes me sad that each of us, every one of us, had our separate premonitions and warnings and still could do nothing to prevent his death. I wondered if a premonition was a blessing or a curse. I was always one who wanted to know the truth—even if painful. So, would I have preferred to not have a premonition? I guess not. The premonition truly was a gift from God's invisible realm that eventually led me to a deeper understanding of life and death itself. Sadly, at the time the premonitions occurred, none of us knew what to think of them or whether to believe them. We are not taught to listen to our souls.

CHAPTER 25

The Psychic Circuit

Having finally linked into the shadow world of the psychic network, I spent the next three years compulsively seeking out psychic mediums and grasping at the momentary solace I found in glimpses of Mikey still alive in another world. I desperately clung to that tenuous connection. I had ten readings with four different psychic mediums, two women and two men. I sat in four of these readings alone. Mike and Peggie and sometimes her fiancé, joined me in the remaining six. Although all of the psychics offered telephone readings, I wanted to actually be in the room to see if I felt Mikey's presence. All I can say is that the energy in the room felt charged. I finally resorted to having three telephone readings since it was becoming difficult and expensive to journey so far and so often. I have tape recordings of all the readings except for the two with a local psychic who did not provide that service.

I stored each tape recording away in my closet in a special box labeled "Spirit Communications with Mikey." For years, that box sat on a shelf above Mikey's once crisply-ironed shirts still hanging on their original hangers. The box sat next to his worn baseball glove still holding his baseball and his scuffed hiking boots he had worn hiking in the Grand Canyon one winter with his cousin. I had never listened to any of these tapes until more than a decade later. Although my memory of those readings was positive, there was also a tinge of disappointment after each session. It just wasn't enough. I hadn't realized yet that nothing would ever be enough. We felt an aura of peace as we left each session, but what had happened was indirect and invisible. It was like listening to a narrator on the radio who claims to be relaying information from a person standing silently next to him. Can you ever be sure there really is a person standing next to him? Maybe there is no one standing next to him, and he is just making it all up. Maybe there is someone standing there, but he is translating incorrectly. I know I am suggesting skepticism, but I never really doubted that something unique was happening. The information that came through fit too well to have been all been fabricated, and there was nothing blatantly wrong.

What surprised me the most as I now listened to these tapes was that I found their contents more soothing than I did during the actual reading. As I sat in my office late at night listening on my headphones, I now felt Mikey's presence was there in those sessions. After listening, I would go to sleep feeling at peace. I would wake up the next morning feeling like I had visited him in my dreams. I don't remember that degree of serenity at the original sessions. It is almost as if I truly didn't hear the message at the time. I must have been in some kind of panic state, like a drowning person grasping for anything to hang onto while being swept away in a raging current. In those days, I remember running from place to place trying to find him. He had ridden out one day on his bike and had never come back. Although it was irrational, I was always looking for him. Sometimes I thought I saw him across the parking lot going into a store, or riding alone along the bike path that paralleled the highway, or ahead of me in a car disappearing into traffic. He was always just out of reach. Then a strange thing started to happen. Every young man became him. I saw him in the young men on TV being sent to war. I saw him in the wounded soldier trying to walk again. I even saw him in a group of children on TV who were disembarking a bus to attend an adoption fair in Chicago. He was holding the hand of his little blond sister hoping to be found by parents who would love them. I wanted them! He was everywhere and nowhere. It was such a strange feeling. I think I was in a peculiar state of grief, too shattered to understand the significance of anything except that Mikey was gone from my life. I wanted him back. That is all I really wanted. These readings could not bring him back, at least not physically.

While listening to all of these taped sessions, I realized that the very first reading (described above) and the last were the most remarkable. Yet, each reading had bright jewels of validation. However, in subsequent readings with the same psychic, there was a lot of extraneous filler in an attempt to satisfy me and fill up the allotted time. The filler consisted of helpful advice dealing with grief of the sort we had already learned from The Compassionate Friends. Sometimes there were religious explanations of the afterlife, which were nice, but nothing more. I did not find fault with these digressions and considered them to be necessary breathing room. It had to be difficult maintaining communication in an altered state for a full hour. The psychics would often relay that sort of advice as if it was coming from Mikey, which did not have the ring of truth. They were likely biding time until more impressions could be channeled. I didn't mind these gaps because I also needed to absorb what was happening.

An example of a jewel of validation that popped up in the midst of filler was when the psychic reported that Mikey was reciting the 23rd Psalm. "The Lord is my shepherd; I shall not want. He maketh me to lie down in green pastures; He leadeth me beside the still waters. He restoreth my soul." We all gasped in amazement, because we recited the 23rd Psalm repeatedly during those early days. We always held hands and recited it together over his grave, and often whispered it alone when we felt the need. Mikey's birthday was the 23rd, which made the Psalm seem appropriate. A skeptic might say this was a safe guess, but it was significant to us.

Having gone to four different psychics, I could also cross-check what they each said. I expected that some of the same information would come up independently, and it did. One small example of independent information: two psychics said Mikey sat next to me when I was driving. That might seem like an easy guess, except that it felt familiar and relevant to me. This information was not said to my husband or to my daughter who drive every day. I, on the other hand, don't like to drive and rarely do. But when I did drive alone, I always had the comforting feeling that Mikey was sitting in the front seat next to me. It reminded me of the time I picked him up from Camp Mishawaka in Minnesota one summer, and we drove home together in our green Ford LTD. Out in the middle of nowhere, the car's old radiator blew in a dramatic spout of white steam. Mikey threw up his hands in a "now, what!" gesture. We couldn't call for help because cell phones weren't invented yet. It had rained the previous night, so there was water in the drainage ditch alongside the road. We got the brilliant idea to fill a plastic jug with water from the ditch and pour it into the radiator. We were able to drive again for a while until we had to fill it again. We could see a small town in the distance. Our goal was to get there. When we got there we had the ruptured hose replaced. So, now when I drive alone I always feel him quietly sitting next to me in case I have another emergency.

The two male psychics were the only ones able to describe the accident. I still had questions about what had actually happened and hoped for answers. Although the most detailed description was in our last reading, which I will relate later, the Reverend K described the accident from Mikey's perspective in enough detail it gave him credibility with me. Although I have omitted much of the superfluous portions of the reading, there were astonishing portions that I have pondered over the years.

The reading with Reverend K. took place on May 8, 1995. He began the session by saying a protective prayer in a rather strange singsong manner. Almost immediately he said he felt a pain in his chest. He said he felt as though he couldn't breathe, that his head was hurting, and that he felt a snap in his neck.

Reverend K.: It is a weird sensation, almost like a body blow. I feel a sharp pain here in my neck. I am feeling like I am around the body watching the whole thing happen. He didn't feel any pain because he immediately stepped out of his body. Then he couldn't get back into his body. He was so shocked! He was literally scared out of his body.

He was sorry he left. He had no idea how many people would be disrupted by it. He was surprised how many people were at his funeral.

At this point I heard a window crack in the room where the reading took place. It was a warm day. The windows continued to crack periodically during the entire hour.

Reverend K.: That was him.

Jane: That was him? I heard that sound all the time after he died. There was a picture hanging over my couch in the den that was cracking whenever I was lying there. I always wondered what it was.

Reverend K.: That is spirit doing that. That is what they do to show that they are present. I feel a younger male presence around him. There was someone who took it very hard. Does he have a brother?

Jane: No. That would be his friend, Eric. They looked so much alike they could have been brothers.

Reverend K.: It is a brotherly feeling. He is still taking it hard. You could drop him a card. He didn't leave early. He had fulfilled what he came to accomplish. We choose our parents. We also choose what we decide our lesson will be. He was a spiritually in-tune young man, a very gentle spirit. There is a young woman, as well, who is still taking it very hard.

Jane: That would be his wife.

Reverend K.: Do you have contact with her?

Jane: No. She really wanted nothing to do with us after Mikey died. I think she took it so hard, she took it out on us … actually on me.

Reverend K.: Just know that was her grief. Some people shut completely down in grief.

Jane: Yes, I agree. I was clinging onto everyone and everything, and she was pushing everything away, including us. It was almost like a bitter divorce.

Reverend K.: Hmmm … She was kind of an odd duck, anyway. I see a child there with him. A beautiful little boy. Did she have a miscarriage? I feel it may have been just a conception and then lost.

There was just something unusual about her period. It was a very short life.

> *I was astonished at this comment! One time when Mikey came home for a visit with his wife, he seemed very frustrated when he came in the door. He mumbled something … "she's bleeding." I wasn't sure what he was talking about. I thought then that it might have been that he thought she was pregnant, but she wasn't and he was disappointed. I didn't question him as he really didn't say anything directly to me. This confirmed that my vague impression was not just my imagination. I was going to be a grandmother!*

Reverend K.: How is Grandma doing? I have a strange feeling with her, like my head is woozy, like she is losing her balance. I feel my head bobbing around. She will not be here a whole lot longer, and it actually will be a blessing. She is a feisty lady. She is frustrated that she can't get up and go. I feel she is having a hard time because she feels she wants to be there with him.

> *I thought this description was incredible. My mother had suffered for a long time from a condition that affected her balance. She was unable to walk without support and eventually was confined to a wheelchair. She told me that her head felt woozy! She also grieved deeply over Mikey, wishing she had died instead of him. She told me she wanted to be buried next to him.*

Reverend K.: He is waiting for her. When it is time for Grandma, he will be there for her.

> *Four-and-a-half years after this psychic reading my dear mother died, just two days before her 90th birthday. We had already purchased the party decorations for this milestone birthday. I clearly remember the morning she died. I was sitting in a technical meeting at work. There were about thirty people packed into a conference room where someone was diagramming the way to make some particular telephone feature work. I was at the far end of the conference table opposite the open door. While I was listening to the presentation, I glanced over to the open doorway. At that moment, I got a mental image of Mikey rushing past the doorway with a notebook tucked under his arm. He was beaming and seemed to be saying that he was late for an*

important appointment. I smiled at the charming image of my last-minute Mike. After the meeting finally ended, I returned to my office, where I received a call that my mother had died. It was not expected. She had been in the hospital the week before because of a sore on her leg that would not heal. She was given all kinds of precautionary tests while under intensive treatment. My sister Clarissa later told me our mother often called out to Mikey as she drifted in and out of sleep during her stay at the hospital. After a week everything appeared to be fine, so she was released from the hospital. However, unknown to me, she was rushed back to the hospital that morning because she had blacked out. My sister Carole called an ambulance to take her back to the hospital as a precaution. She left home protesting angrily that she didn't need to go back to the hospital. She was a very feisty and determined lady. When she got to the hospital she had a stroke and died. They were unable to resuscitate her. I have always believed Mikey got the news she was coming and was rushing to meet her. I know she would have been delighted!

I knew then that no matter what, I would see him again. My dear son would be there to meet me when I die. I will be overjoyed. He is there waiting. With notebook and all, he will be the first to welcome each of us home.

CHAPTER 26

The Wedding

On August 19,1995, our daughter married a man she met at work. He had been divorced about five years and had custody of his two preteen sons. The fact that he had custody seemed to indicate to me that he had a good character. More importantly, he seemed head-over-heels in love with Peggie. Everyone in the family had been waiting for the day that Miss Peggie would marry. At age thirty-four she said she had finally found the right one. After two years of unrelenting sadness, our hearts soared with happiness as we planned her wedding day. I have always loved weddings. They are such jubilant celebrations—full of promise! I enjoyed being the mother of the bride, shopping for her beautiful lace wedding dress, hair ornaments, and pearl jewelry. We went to a small bridal shop in an old building near the Fox River where we selected the two bridesmaids' dresses in peach satin with matching pumps. We seriously collected "something old, something new, something borrowed, and something blue." Instead of a box for the gift envelopes, we painted an antique birdcage white and decorated it with her favorite ivy. We each selected music for the disc jockey. One song my husband and I chose was a poignant piece from *Fiddler on the Roof.*

> Sunrise, sunset
> Swiftly fly the years
> One season following another
> Laden with happiness and tears.

Peggie and her fiancé put a lot of thought into creating a beautiful ceremony and elegant reception. They chose Bible verses about love as their theme:

> Love is patient and kind. Love knows no limit to its endurance, no end to its trust. Love still stands when all else has fallen.

They wrote special vows that included his two boys. Peggie's little cousin Karrie Anne who was just five years old was the flower girl. She stole everyone's heart as she scattered rose petals down the church aisle ahead of the bride. Her proud parents, Karen and Rick, stood up in their pew to take pictures of her. As the organ triumphantly began "The Wedding March," all heads turned to watch the radiant bride and her father as they linked arms and began the slow, stylized walk down the aisle. Everything was breathtakingly perfect. Although they had a professional photographer, I took a lot of pictures of the entire day. I had taken informal and candid pictures as well as the traditional poses. I was flattered that the bride and groom liked my photographs better. The heat of that August day was a sweltering, causing our fancy clothes to cling to our bodies as we strolled in the beautiful gardens outside the reception hall. All the surrounding towns had reported heavy rains and flooding, but it did not rain on us. My good friend from work was unable to get out of her flooded subdivision, but almost everyone came to this long-anticipated occasion. Mikey's good friends, Eric and Cara, drove all the way from Angola with their young daughter to join the celebration at the reception. I knew in my heart that Eric had come to stand in for Mikey—our fallen soldier. Eric's presence was especially important because Cristal neither came nor responded to the invitation in any way.

Peggie and I at her wedding

I will never forget the ambience in the ballroom that evening. It was brimming with conviviality—the music playing, everyone dancing and drinking toasts to the newlyweds. I danced the traditional dance with my new son-in-law. His mother warmly welcomed me to their family, hugging me and holding both my hands in hers. She commented that the air felt filled with love, and it surely did. Love suffused the air, reaching into every corner of the room from the parquet dance floor up to the crystal chandeliers. It even enhanced the brilliance of the spinning disco ball sprinkling dots of light like stars across the walls. It flowed across the room and around the tables adorned with roses and soft candlelight. It caressed the guests, nudging and nestling into their hearts. Peggie said she felt that Mikey was there. He indeed was there, contributing to that feeling of perfect love, so full of hope for the future. For the first time since Mikey had died, I felt there was a reason to go on living.

We built a big house along the Illinois Prairie Path shortly after the wedding. It had four bedrooms! I hoped to have grandchildren sleeping over. I started collecting children's books. I envisioned myself reading bedtime stories to my grandchildren. I thought of all the things that fascinated me as a child: fairy tales, constellations, ghost stories, and Nancy Drew mysteries. What a delight it would be to share these with my own grandchildren. And my husband could take them fishing, show them how to tend a garden, or raise a puppy. Of course, there were already two step-grandchildren. The older boy was still a little difficult and resentful of his parents' divorce and his father's re-marriage. Oddly enough, this was in spite of the fact that his mother had already remarried. However, the problem seemed surmountable with time and patience. The younger boy adored Peggie and was a perfect match to her in temperament. He was artistic like she was. He was in touch with his feelings and even at his young age he understood the nuances of poetry. He liked the idea of our being his grandparents. It all seemed like a wonderful new beginning for our family.

Unfortunately, some trouble in the marriage began soon after the wedding. Of course, one must always expect a period of adjustment, especially with children already present. The older boy had long been favored and coddled because he had health issues. Using his edge of always being able to get attention focused on him, he showed resentment to Peggie, which did not help the situation. At the same time, the younger son absolutely adored Peggie, but it didn't seem to matter as much. Peggie soon found out that her husband had a violent temper. Peggie hadn't dated him long enough before they married to see that side of him. I saw the first hint of trouble when he had a meltdown at the rehearsal dinner, the night before the wedding. I was shocked, but everyone seemed to chalk it up to jitters. On the whole, though, things seemed to be good at first. They seemed very much in love and behaved caringly toward one another. As part of their plan to have children together, he had his vasectomy reversed shortly after they were married He even joined us for two of the psychic readings. In one reading, he surprised me when he said he felt Mikey's hand on his shoulder more than once. In the reading with the first psychic, Peggie's having a child was a dominant and recurring theme as we continued to see this psychic. She was convinced that Mikey wanted to come back to the family as Peggie's child. To my surprise, the theme of Peggie having a child also came up strongly and persistently in our last reading with a famous male psychic. However, he felt that Mikey would be a guardian angel for the child.

There are some things you just take for granted about life. I always expected that we would be grandparents. We married young, had children young. There was plenty of time for us to have grandchildren, even great-grandchildren. Each of us always had so much love and learning to give to our children. My husband was an industrious and productive person, probably because he had known poverty as a child. He grew up in Europe during the devastation of WWII. Although he lived in the foothills of the beautiful Austrian Alps, he remembered being hungry all the time. As a child he had raised rabbits so his family would have food to eat. He collected branches in the woods to heat their small, dirt-floor house. When there were scant jobs, he was fortunate to find an apprenticeship to a baker and began to fully support himself at the age of fourteen. He was diligently saving his money to buy a motor scooter, when his father told him his quota number finally came up and he could go to America. At the age of eighteen he boarded an old English troop carrier, *The General Langfith,* with twenty-three dollars in his pocket. On the voyage over he found work in the ship's kitchen washing dishes and earned another four dollars. Despite being trained as a professional baker, he earned very little money on his first job, even though he was working fourteen hours a day, seven days a week.

We met in the bakery where he worked and where I got a summer job before heading away to my first year at Purdue University on a scholarship. I thought he was an angel when I first saw him. His hair was longer then, as was the style in Europe. He later said he thought I was such a beautiful young lady with my long, dark hair. He didn't think he had a chance with me. That summer he took me to a Hungarian picnic where we danced the *chardash* like gypsies. He kissed my hand afterward. He almost melted my mother's Hungarian heart, but she protested that I was "college material." My father disapproved of my dating because I was the academic high achiever of the family, and he didn't believe women could combine family and career. My older sister had quit college to get married, and he was afraid I would do the same. However, the harder my parents tried to separate us, the more we clung together. I was nineteen and he was twenty-two when we married. He had saved four hundred dollars that we spent on a refrigerator, stove, and kitchen table. We also had a car payment for the yellow Ford Fairlane 500 that he raced down Route 41 to Purdue every weekend to visit me. Over the many years of our marriage, we both had worked hard. I stayed home when the children were small and enjoyed every aspect of those precious years. During that same time I also earned a Bachelor of Science degree from Purdue University. With my degree I began a career in the telecommunications industry when the children entered high school. Mike opened his own very successful bakery business. We built a comfortable life, which we hoped to share with grandchildren. Peggie said she wanted a child, and I knew she would make a wonderful mother. She was kind and loyal. She was sensitive to the feelings of others, yet also had a good head on her shoulders. She had a wonderful sense of humor. She would make a great mother. I was very hopeful that there would be a grandchild. It was our last hope, our last chance to bring our family back to life.

CHAPTER 27

Another Death in the Family

In the early months of 1996 I discovered a psychic who lived in my home state. Her name was Greta. She was a psychic detective who helped police solve cases of missing persons and murder. She was considered one of the top psychics in the country.[16] Although her specialty was not spirit communication, her office staff said she would be willing to do a reading for me. She knew nothing about me except my name and my wish to contact my son. She only did readings by telephone without tape recordings, but I have never forgotten certain details of the session.

She began by telling me I had two children, a boy and a girl. She said she saw them sitting on a cloud before they were born, and that they chose us as parents. Strikingly, her description was exactly the same way I had envisioned them before they were born. She said the love between my son and me was a perfect love. Those were the exact words she used. What a wonderful thing to recognize. I have found such comfort in those words over the years. The only thing she could tell me about Mikey's accident was that she saw something cross his path. It reminded me of the shadow that fell across my soul the day he died. She told me he was not happy. In the many after-death communication stories I had read up to that time, the deceased were always happy and contented, forgiving and at peace. When she said Mikey was not happy, my heart fell; but I understood why. He had finally gotten his life all together. He wanted to be with here with all of us. His reasons for being unhappy were obvious.

Occasionally, Greta came up to the Chicago area to visit a relative and offered readings in person. I was notified when she was coming and was thrilled to make an appointment. She had asked everyone to bring a gift of winter gloves for the children in orphanages in the area. Six weeks later, with the gift of gloves in hand, I arrived at her hotel for my appointment. I was surprised to find that no one else was waiting to see her. When I knocked on the door, her assistant informed me that Greta had cancelled all her appointments because her relative was in the hospital. They said they had tried to notify me but were unable to because I had an unlisted telephone number. I was disappointed and started to walk away. To my surprise, Greta summoned me in to do my reading anyway. That was the mark of a true psychic—a person who listens to the call of the universe. I had not gotten the cancellation message, so to her way of thinking that meant she was supposed to give me a reading.

Greta told me that Mikey had a message for me. He said that everything about Egypt was true. When I looked a little perplexed, she simply stated, "That is what he wants me to tell you." This was the only time during any of my readings that information about what he was currently doing came through. It was so characteristic of him. One of the things I always loved about him was that he was always telling me something new he had learned. It started when he was a preschooler teaching himself arithmetic, and it never stopped. He was a history buff, so this message was totally in line with his interests. It had the feel of a genuine communication.

Greta then foretold of another death in our family. She said she saw the doors of a funeral parlor opening. She said it would be a male. Because Peggie's father-in-law was very ill at the time, I asked if it was the death of an older man. She said, "No, it is a younger man with a hidden health problem." I was perplexed. I mentally scanned all the young males in the family and could not imagine who it could be. The following month another psychic also briefly mentioned an eminent death in the family. She also described the doors to a funeral parlor opening. However, she could not offer any specifics. The thought of another death in the family was too much to contemplate, so I put it out of my mind.

That very year, on the day after Christmas, my sister Clarissa called me in the middle of the night to tell me her daughter Karen's husband had died unexpectedly of a heart attack. Since it was an unknown condition the news was shocking. Rick was only thirty-seven years old, a loving husband and devoted father to his six-year-old daughter Karrie Anne, the flower girl at Peggie's wedding. Rick was one of the cousins who had carried Mikey's coffin three years earlier. His death sent our family into a tailspin of stunned disbelief once again. Our family had lost yet another good young man in his prime.

We immediately went to Karen's side to offer what support we could. I couldn't stop crying; it was just all so sad once again. A priest and a pastor spoke at the funeral service, but it was the eulogies of his family members that truly revealed all that had been lost at this young man's death. Karen's brother Eddie tearfully noted, "He was a good and decent man."

Little Karrie Anne kept looking into the casket and innocently asking her mother, "Why can't someone else die instead?" While Peggie and I sat in the front row at the service, a young woman came up to speak to us. She knelt in front of Peggie and said she had also lost her brother some years ago in a motorcycle accident. She spoke of all the agony she had gone through at the time and said the only thing that pulled her out of it was when she married and had a child. She said so many things about her child reminded her of her dead brother that she felt his spirit had come to life again in her little boy. She encouraged Peggie to have a child to ease her loss. To my surprise, Peggie really didn't seem responsive to this young woman who had suffered a similar tragedy and was now taking the time to comfort her. I began to sense that something was wrong, but I tried to not dwell on it. There just had been too much sadness in our lives already.

Over the years I've felt a special bond with Karen because we'd both suffered a tragic and untimely loss. We often spoke of ways to deal with others who didn't understand grief. I had to laugh when I heard that she had thrown a new boyfriend out of her house in the middle of the night when he told her she needed to "get over it." She once revealed to me that during the six months before her husband had died, he told her he was "speaking" often with his own deceased father. I have come to believe that this is a sign that someone is preparing to cross over. As the years have passed Karen has done a wonderful job raising her daughter on her own. Karrie Anne is now a well-adjusted college student, studying music. This young man who died too soon would be proud of them both.

Karen recently sent me this beautiful note:

> My dear Aunt Jane,
>
> Please know that I feel your sadness every day. Both Karrie and I love you and Uncle Mike very much. I will never forget that you both came to me right away when you received the news about Rick. You sent us a beautiful card, with the saying that we placed on his headstone, "It matters not how long a star shines; what is remembered is the brightness of its light."
>
> Love,
>
> Karen & Karrie

CHAPTER 28

The Gold Standard Psychic

At the end of April 1997, I got a pleasant and unexpected call that there was a last-minute opening for an appointment with George Anderson. He was touring the country and would be doing readings at a hotel in Cincinnati, Ohio, the following week. Someone had cancelled their appointment, so it was very short notice. "Did we want the appointment?" This was the very George Anderson I saw on TV right after Mikey died! It was the program that started me on my quest to communicate with Mikey through a medium. George Anderson was the gold standard by which all other mediums were judged. He had been tested scientifically. Books had been written about him. Now he was available at a hotel within driving distance! I could not believe my good fortune. Surely, Mikey had pulled some strings to make this happen after all these years. I grabbed the appointment without a second thought and scrambled to make arrangements to travel.

Mike and I made the journey to Cincinnati by van—together with my daughter and her husband. We arrived early. Since it was a beautiful, sunny, spring day, we strolled around the hotel gardens where the flowering trees bloomed. Many people were milling about—some waiting for appointments. To pass the time until our appointment, we decided to have lunch in the hotel restaurant. I couldn't help noticing that one of the waiters bore a striking resemblance to Mikey, but I didn't comment on it. Then Peggie's husband, who had only seen Mikey in pictures, pointed out the waiter and asked if he looked like Mikey. We were all astounded by the resemblance. It was hard not to stare at him. It seemed as though Mikey had made his first physical appearance! When it was finally time for our appointment, only Peggie and I chose to sit for the reading. I think these sessions were making my husband too sad. They made him long for Mikey even more, so he didn't want to join us. He also told me our first reading was very healing and was enough for him. The men waited for us outside in the gardens as we rushed back to the hotel lobby.

George Anderson's assistant met Peggie and me in the hallway outside his suite. We were escorted through several doorways into a large, softly-lit room and invited to sit on a comfortable couch. They did not record sessions for clients, but allowed us to bring our own recorder. I set it on the floor by my feet and turned it on as soon as George Anderson came into the room. I had given my name when I made the appointment, but that was the only information Mr. Anderson had about us. My credit card had only my name on it. My phone number was listed only in my name. So, my name is all he had. I say this because my husband's name is the same as my son's, and he could have guessed Mikey's name that way. But, he didn't have my husband's name. We obviously had come for a spirit communication, but he knew nothing at all about our situation or anything about the person we wished to contact. Further, he would not have been able to assume that Peggie and I were mother and daughter because we do not look alike.

George insisted that we give him absolutely no information beforehand or during the reading. He wanted none of the items often requested by other mediums: no pictures, no names, no birthdays, nothing. We were only allowed a minimum response, just enough for him to stay on track. Because he was basically starting at zero, he had to spend more time figuring things out from the impressions and symbols he received from the spirits. He would often come back again and again to something in order to figure it out. His intent was to prove to his clients that he was actually communicating with the spirits of their loved ones. He sat facing us in a rigid wooden chair about ten feet away. Just as I had seen on TV four years earlier, he randomly scratched on a notepad on his lap as he spoke to us. He tended to look down at his notepad as a way to focus his thoughts—looking up at us occasionally. He had a humble manner. I have transcribed all the critical portions of the reading. I've also included much of the "filler," because it helped me finally to see the forest and not the trees. After four years and ten psychic readings, I finally was ready to hear the greater message: there is life after death.

CHAPTER 29

The Last Psychic Reading

May 2, 1997: Spirit communication with George Anderson, Cincinnati, Ohio.

George: Okay. I can feel someone is coming in already *(chuckled)* so we don't waste any time! And away we go! Just say "yes" or "no" or "I understand." But certainly think with me. Sometimes I don't understand what they are talking about, and I will throw the ball in your lap. If you understand what they mean, then you can say "I understand" without explaining anything to me. Okay? First of all, certainly a male presence has come into the room. Now, a lot of times I won't be looking at you, but I can hear you. So, you can respond.

Jane: Yes. *(softly)*

George: A male presence has come into the room, two as a matter of fact. A female presence, as well. And another one (female). So I have at least four people have shown up so far. They do give me the feeling of family, family by love or by choice. Certainly, there is a family link. Now, they also link you both in a family sense *(nodding to Peggie and me)*. Is that correct?

Jane/Peggie: Yes.

George: Someone in the crowd is saying, "Dad is here." Does that make sense? Is it correct that your dad has passed … or father-in-law?

Jane: Yes.

George: I have the feeling of your biological father. Has your biological dad passed?

Jane: Yes. *(My father died over twenty years earlier. I felt close to him growing up and always missed him.)*

George: Somebody keeps saying, "Dad is here." Wait. So, has your biological dad passed?

Jane: Yes.

George: Okay. But I heard it twice. Well, let me go with what I am feeling. I am getting the feeling of your biological father. Wait. But, I heard it twice. So, is there a step-dad or something? Well, let me go with what I am feeling. I am hearing, "Dad is here." I am getting the feeling of your biological father. I am getting, "Dad is here" twice. So, I am going to leave it alone. One of the males here is definitely your biological dad, but there may be someone else coming with him.

Someone is talking about the younger male that has passed on. Wait a second. The younger male keeps pushing dad. Does that make sense?

Peggie: *(laughs)* Yes!

George: This is where I am getting the mix-up, because he keeps telling me to push the fatherly role. And he keeps saying, "Dad is here" for some reason. Then he tells me to say out loud, "Push the fatherly role."

Peggie: *(laughing)* Yes, it makes sense to me!

> *She told me later that she felt Mikey was pushing the fatherly role on her husband. He wanted to be born to Peggie, so he was telling her to push the fatherly role on her husband.*

George: Someone is talking about the son that passed on. Does that make sense? There are too many people talking at one time. Someone is talking about, "Push the fatherly role." Then someone talks about the son that has passed on ... hmmm. Both of you would know him. There is a son that passed on and both of you know him. Okay. I am going to have to assume that one of you has lost a son? Is that correct? *(looking at both of us)*

Jane: Yes.

George: Yourself?

Jane: Yes.

George: That would be the younger male. Your son is telling you he is there with your dad. Whether they knew each other or not, he is there with your dad. But wait a minute. Her son *(indicating me)* keeps coming to you *(looking at Peggie)*, so you know him, yes? He wants to tell you that although he keeps focusing on his mom for the moment, you are not being ignored.

Peggie: *(laughs, like of course she knew that)*

George: Wait a second, now I am confused. He is the one saying, "Push the fatherly role." Do you understand?

Peggie: Yeah!

George: As long as you understand! I refuse to let you explain, but he is saying, "Push the fatherly role."

Peggie: I think I understand!

George: Wait. He also puts a big heart in front of you *(indicating Peggie)*. Does that mean you and he are family? But family by blood. When he puts a big heart in front of you it is out of fondness. Wait, he keeps saying, "Sister."

Peggie: Yes.

George: He keeps speaking of children. Does that make sense?

Peggie: Yes! *(laughing, smiling)*

George: Is it correct that he does not have children? He says, "I do not have children."

Jane/Peggie: Yes.

George: However, you do? *(to Peggie)*

Peggie: No. *(pause)* I want children.

George: This is why he keeps saying, "Push the fatherly role," because he would be around your children as a father figure. Apparently, it could mean that in the not too distance future you must have children. Now there is a feeling of his explaining that this would be significant to you. I also see St. Philomena around you, who is the patroness of a happy birth. So apparently, there is going to be a happy birth up ahead. I take it that you are not in a family way now, but ahead you will be. Again, he is saying, "Push the fatherly role." You are married now?

Peggie: Yes. *(laughing happily again)*

George: Apparently, something is on the horizon. Maybe you are going to start a family. There has to be some depth to this. He extends you white roses and congratulates you on a happy birth up ahead.

He keeps stating that he is all right. That must make sense for some reason. He also speaks of his own dad. His dad is here on the earth, correct? He keeps calling out to his father, as well. His dad suffers in silence over his passing. Would you say that is true?

Jane: Yes.

George. Again he says, "Push the fatherly role." When he said, "Dad is here," he is calling out to his dad. "Tell Dad you heard from me and that I send my love." Whether he believes in this or not, your son could care less. He says, "It's the message I am trying to convey, not the belief system, because Dad is going to have to show up here some day and find out that I am right as usual. *(laughter)* You can tell him I said so." *(laughter)* He knows how much his father loves him and misses him. "Tell him I love him, too, and I am closer to him than he can imagine. He can sit back and say this is all a bunch of bull, fine, but he will find out I am right some day." Yes, his dad does suffer in silence over the passing. Your son speaks of a tragic passing. Is that correct?

Jane: Yes.

George: He also puts it under the umbrella of an accident. Is that correct?

Jane/Peggie: Yes.

George: He keeps stating that it is no one's fault. Does that make sense?

Jane: Yes.

George: There is a depth to what he is saying, because I feel it is at the bottom of the ocean. It is no one's fault. No one is to be blamed. Does that make sense?

Jane: Yes.

George: You might think otherwise, but that is what he says. He says, remember, it is my opinion, my perspective. Now, he shows a vehicle-type accident. Is it correct that he is in a vehicle-type accident? Or a vehicle is involved? It might not be a car, but it is a vehicle of some sort. He keeps telling me he is in a vehicle-type accident. Vehicle being the key word.

Jane/Peggie: Yes.

George: He claims he does not suffer on his passing. He is gone from one moment to the next. I also feel pressure to my head. There must also have been some kind of head injury. I don't want to sound graphic, but I have the feeling of my brains being bashed in. I see St. Joseph appearing in the room, who is the patron of a happy death. Your son passes happily to the hereafter in spite of the circumstances. He also speaks of home, or coming home when this occurs?

Jane: Umm … no.

George: Okay. Let me leave that go. This may not be your home; it may be near his own home. He is near his home when it occurs because he keeps bringing it up. I also feel I am falling. Apparently he is tossed. He is catapulted a bit. Falling, not from a building. But I am falling. He is talking about being exposed. Is the vehicle exposed? Was he driving a motorcycle or something? Because he says he is exposed. I think he means a motorcycle. Because, it's not like he is in a tank, obviously. I don't know what he means that he is exposed. I am thinking he means a motorcycle. It must mean something where he is exposed. He feels it contributes to the accident. Because of the fact that he is exposed. He is not protected to the degree like he would be in a car, for example. Is this correct?

> *A witness said that he was hit by the car and thrown high up into the air, catapulted is a good word. Then he fell to the ground. The bicycle hit the metal pole of the street sign and left a mark on it according to the report from Packer Engineering.*

Jane/Peggie: Yes.

George: Yeah, this contributes to the goriness of the tragedy. Also, there is something that injured the neck. I am getting the feeling of an injury to the neck. Is this correct?

Jane/Peggie: Yes.

> *(Mikey's neck was broken. You can hear us using tissues as we cry throughout this segment.)*

George: Yes, I get the feeling from the neck up was the dominant injury, causing instantaneous death. This is why he states that he is all right. He says don't feel that his life was snuffed out. It has continued somewhere else as if he packed his bags and moved to a different country. Yes, he knows you would much rather have him here, but this is the best he can do. "I am not dead; I am alive." Yes, his physical body is gone. You buried him, whatever. But the essence of him has survived.

He claims he has come in dreams. Apparently, this is not the first time he has come to you. He gives thanks for the memorial, and also for the planting. Does that make sense?

Jane: Yes. A memorial, yes.

George: And the planting. Someone must have planted in his memory. If it wasn't you, then it could have been someone else, because he is insisting.

> *It is interesting that the psychic didn't let this go. Then I remembered that Mimi, a family friend, had a tree planted for him in Israel. Also, my husband is a gardener and has planted much for him.*

Obviously, good things have been done in his name. His name is inscribed, he states.

> *His wife set up a scholarship at Purdue Calumet in his name, and we have contributed to it ever since. We also bought a paver with his name inscribed on it at the on the new walkway at Purdue Calumet.*

Yes, he speaks about a hit with this vehicle. Would that be true?

Jane/Peggie: Yes.

George: I feel there is a hit and a throw. A crash, like hitting into something. Then I am catapulted or thrown. It's funny, but it is almost as if he didn't think he would live to a great age. Yeah, he doesn't seem surprised to be in the hereafter. It's almost like he knew he wouldn't live to be a great age. It was almost like he was trying to get all his work done. I keep getting a feeling of him being in a hurry. Again, as your son states, remember that he is an individual as we all are, on his own spiritual odyssey. It could be that he got his work done sooner than we all have and that is why he is there and we are all still here. As he states when get your work done, you move on. If you get your work done ahead of schedule then you have to find a way out. In his case he got his work done ahead of schedule. He might have been scheduled to pass on at fifty, for example. Yet, he got his work done sooner. And the evidence is that you can recall him trying to get everything done. You almost want to say to him, "What's the hurry?" Because he knew in the back of his mind that his time was coming. It is like someone trying to get everything ready when they are getting ready to go on a trip. So he knew his time was coming.

> *I always felt he was in a hurry about everything. He filled every moment of his day his whole life. But I especially felt those last weeks that he was in a hurry. He was planting his garden, he wanted those bricks for his garden "pretty quick," and all those other things that made me feel he had a premonition.*

Why do I keep seeing gems in front of you? Does that mean anything? Maybe it is a symbol. It could be a symbol of a spiritual blessing. Maybe you thought of him as a real gem, so he is showing you gems. You look upon him as a jewel. As much as you thought he was a gem or a jewel in this world, he is a gem in the hereafter.

We smiled at this, because this is exactly how we felt about him.

He speaks of a pet that passed on, he is there with him. *(Spike, his dog)* He also singularizes himself. That can mean he is the only son, or he is the eldest or the youngest. Do any of those apply? Is this correct that he is the only son?

Jane: Yes.

George: That is why it hits home so bad. He jokes that you are the last of the Mohicans. (*to Peggie)* So, I guess you are. Yes?

Peggie: Yes.

George: He puts the book over your head and says, "She is the last of the Mohicans." He must have had a good sense of humor. He is doing this not to make light of your grief, but to let you know he is back to his own self. He is himself again, just living somewhere else. He says, "You think I am far away from you, but we are parallel to each other. The only difference is that your existence is physical and mine is spiritual." But, he says, "You have turned your head and at times and sworn you have seen me."

> *I remember sitting in my black Mercedes at the cemetery a short time after Mikey died. It was raining hard, so I just sat in the car and thought about him. Out of the corner of my eye I thought I saw someone standing there, in the rain, in blue jeans and jacket. Startled, I quickly turned my head, but saw no one. I felt it was Mikey.*

George: You have glimpsed at times into the hereafter. You have been thinking of him and a song comes on the radio that relates to him. You have had evidences of him before today. This is just a confirmation of what you have already experienced. Even if you had never gotten to see me, you could have still said "This might be a coincidence, but ..." This may be a more profound experience, because I certainly don't know you or your circumstances, but as he says there are evidences that they give out. He says sometimes you look too hard for them, but don't. Just let them happen. If you look too hard for them you are going to miss the forest for the trees.

I think you could always depend on your son on being straightforward and telling it like it is. He is not going to come in and BS. He says to both of you, especially to you as a bereaved parent, recognize that this is the worst experience that could come to you in your life. Some people will say you have to get over it, but you will never get over it. He says don't even try. But, don't let your grief be your downfall. If you live to be ninety, it's not going away. It is with you till the day you pass on. Someday it is going to have to come to an end, because someday you will pass on. You will come to his front door, and it will be as if it never happened.

Sometimes you don't know how you are supposed to feel. *(to Peggie)* Sometimes people don't think the loss is as bad on you as on your parents. He knows that sometimes this forces you to suffer in silence. He knows what you are going through. You were close with him. You love each other. You are still going to miss him. It is not going to go away. I can try to give you signs I am here. Still it is second best.

It's very easy for clergy to say it's God's will, it's this or it's that. But they sure as hell wouldn't trade places with you. He says it is not God's will. It is the fulfillment of his own spiritual odyssey. Just as when you fulfill yours, you are out of here. You have to realize you are individual souls. You will understand when you have your life review. Someday, you have to reach that finish line.

Also, your son talks about your mom. Has she passed?

Jane: No.

George: Or your mother-in-law? He says mom and he points it at you, so it would have to be your mother-in-law. He says your dad is there, but he speaks of your in-laws, too. Has your father-in-law passed, also?

Jane: Yes.

> *It was interesting to me that my husband's parents again came into this reading. I had never met either of them, and my husband was not present at the reading.*

George: There is also the strong presence of your grandmother. This would be his great grandmother. This is the grandmother who was uniquely close to you that you recall.

> *I loved my grandmother, my father's mother. She was warm and comforting and made me feel special. She once told me she wished she could have had a little girl like me. I wanted to go live with her. We were alike in some ways, I thought. She wrote poetry and always wished she could have gone to college.*

George: Remember I saw him, plus two males and two females. So, it's your dad, your in-laws, your grandmother, and him. Now, this is the grandmother you knew best, the one who had the most influence in your life growing up.

Your son keeps telling me to tell you both he is happy and at peace and in a safe place. Do not dwell on the fact that you think his life was snuffed out, that he was cheated, that he never had a chance at life. His life has ended in your world, but has continued in another. Again, picture me packing my bags and moving to a different country. He extends pink roses to you and is wishing you a happy Mother's Day. Because he says you feel like only half a mother now. But he says you have one child here and one child in the hereafter. Some people might say, oh, you're not being realistic. He shows me a mule, so he is saying they are asses! I keep seeing spades in front of him. He must have been the type that calls a spade a spade. He tells it like it is.

Again, he asks that you bring these messages to Dad, also. We are not playing favorite child here, but he was a daddy's boy. They were pals as well as father and son. Your husband feels as if he lost a very good friend as well as a son. Plus, he feels it was such a senseless passing. But he says it was just the means of how he gets to the next direction of his life. It is just the means of getting there.

Now, he speaks of a child. I keep feeling a male presence around you. It is possible that your first one will be a boy. I don't mean to sound funny, but I see a recycle bin in front of me. So, apparently a soul is going to recycle. A soul that didn't have the opportunity in the past for whatever reason; it recognizes a new opportunity may come in the future. So, the soul is biding its time until it is time for it to come to pass. I see St. Gerard, the patron saint of motherhood. Apparently there is motherhood in your future.

George: Your husband *(to Jane)* just wishes he would just die. To put it quite bluntly. He suffers in silence. It was like a bolt of lightning. He has been shocked beyond belief. The grief is not going away. However, don't let it be your downfall. It has taken away your fear of death. Your husband in many ways feels his life is over. This is no reflection on either of you, but it was devastating to him.

Also, I don't mean this as an insult, but it has made you kind of flakey. *(speaking to Jane)* It has rattled you emotionally in such a way that you will never be yourself one hundred percent again. That is why he wants you to take the joy home with you tonight and get a good night's sleep. He is not suffering. He is going on with his life. That is why he has given you evidences before today. He says you have to be here until your time is up. You might as well make the most of it.

Your son keeps giving me the feeling that his first name, without telling me, is short. Is this correct? He is showing me eight letters. If the formal first name is eight letters or less that classifies short to me.

Jane: Yes.

George: Also, he speaks of it as being a common first name, at least common enough that I have heard it before. He also says it can be shortened. Is that true?

Jane: Yes.

George: And he is called by the shortened form. And it is connected to the formal first name. One links to the other. Okay. Let's start over. He said, ABCD, and stopped. So, is the first letter of his name beyond the D in the alphabet?

Jane/Peggie: Yes.

George: It is beyond the E, correct?

Jane/Peggie: Yes.

George: He shot to the M. Is it the M?

Jane/Peggie: Yes. *(laughter)*

George: Oh, good! I told him it is Friday, give me a break! I said beyond the D, he said yes, beyond the E, he said yes, then he shot to the M. Circled the M. Has to begin with M.

(laughter)

George: He just said M as in Michael.

Jane/Peggie: Yes.

George: It is Michael? Oh, good. He also states, also called Mike. And at times, Mikey.

Jane/Peggie: Yes … exactly. *(laughing)*

George: Maybe he didn't like Mikey! But, he will do it, only out of love for you. He says, "This is Michael, this is Mike," then I felt like he wanted to make a face, like, "Do I have to really admit this? They called me Mikey." Then he laughed, and he said, "Out of love I do it for you, although you know I hate it."

Jane/Peggie: *(laughing and crying)*

George: It is interesting. He is extending you white roses *(to Peggie)*. Apparently, he wishes you a happy Mother's Day in advance. Unless things change, you will be celebrating your first Mother's Day in 1998. He is acknowledging you as a mother. He says, "He will be named Michael, won't he?"

Peggie: Yes, of course!

George: Why does he keep talking about work? Was he working when this occurred, this tragedy? Was it a work vehicle? Why do I have a feeling of *whump,* like being hit off of it? I feel like I am being catapulted. Is it correct that he was not in a car?

Peggie/Jane: Yes.

George: He does not say car. He is knocked off or hit off this vehicle.

Jane/Peggie: Yes.

George: He also shows me the words "freak accident." It must have been a freak accident. Maybe that is why I am not comprehending clearly what it is. He keeps describing it as a kind of freak accident.

Jane: Yes.

> *It was astounding and heart-wrenching at the same time as he came back to the accident again and again, trying to describe exactly what had occurred. Only I knew how accurate his description was, because I had read the many witness reports from the police and others.*

George: Again, it breaks your hearts even more because he was such a swell guy. You are thinking what a lousy way to go. But he says, again, it was just the means of getting there.

He says in many ways you suffer in silence, also. There are many days that you just want to jump out the window, but you can't. You just want to throw in the towel. You think there is no more purpose here on earth, especially anymore. You are not supposed to be there, yet. It would be better if you fulfill the terms set by you of how you will get there. You are going to understand someday when you do your life review. The sense of fulfillment, satisfaction will make your grief seem minute. It will be as if you never had it. St. Theresa appears as a symbol of perseverance in times of adversity. Someday you will understand.

The best way to deal with depression is to just acknowledge it is there. It isn't going away. Just let it run its course. It's going to come and it's going to go. That's why it is best to keep busy. There is no harm in distracting your mind from the grief. You need things to look forward to. You are not being irreverent. Don't put off doing things because memories always survive, even in the hereafter.

Also, there is a talk of a brother. Does that make sense? Some close male friend who is like a brother? He is calling out to someone he looked upon as a brother. I don't get a name. "Tell him you heard from me!"

Jane: Yes. *(I believe this is a reference to Eric again.)*

George: Your mom is still on the earth and your son calls to her, as well. Your mom feels bad about his passing. She thinks if someone had to go, why couldn't I have gone? I am an old woman and he was young. (*My mother said exactly this.)* "It's because I was finished with my mission." He jokes and says she is taking too long, that is why she is still there. Your dad calls to her as well. Your mom has had a long life and a hard life. Her surviving a grandchild has rattled her cage. She doesn't have faith anymore.

Jane: Yes.

George: Energy cannot be created or destroyed. Your son says anything that has known or experienced love survives, even an animal. If an animal has loved and known love, that causes it to survive. Because it becomes part of what we know as God. If you look in the Bible, God is love and God is light.

He is going to withdraw. I'm done, I'm done. They know they can hold my brain only so long. We have to back off. In any case, Michael, he jokes, says, "Mikey," is embracing you both with love, and to his dad, too, and his grandmother, family, and friends. Tell them you heard from me and he is at peace. Feel a peace about his passing. Until we meet again. Until we all meet again he sends his love to you.

("Until we meet again" is what I added to his headstone.)

George: He sounds like a character!

CHAPTER 30

Divorce

Everything was pointing to our daughter having a child and our becoming grandparents. It came up again and again in the psychic readings. Peggie now seemed enthusiastic about the prospect of becoming a mother. She even made a promise to me that we would not leave this earth before we were grandparents. After our devastating loss, we were given a glimmer of hope that there was a way to rebuild our family and find joy again. I started reminiscing about those priceless years when my children were babies. I remembered rocking them to sleep, singing lullabies and feeling their soft skin and silken hair against my face. I imagined Peggie enjoying that same blessing. The prospect of such joy after such misery would be nothing less than miraculous. In *The Prophet*, Kahlil Gibran tells us that sorrow carves out a place to fill with joy.[17] If that is true, our joy would be great, indeed.

When having a grandchild became a real possibility, I convinced myself that this was how we could recover from Mikey's tragic death. It could provide a pathway to happiness on so many levels. I had always been curious about reincarnation. A child born as predicted by the psychics—who claimed the spirit of Mikey wanted to be reborn into the family—would bolster the truth of reincarnation. In the book *Return from Heaven*, Carol Bowman documented stories about children who had died very young and returned to the same family. As intriguing as that idea was, it was not the reason I thought having a grandchild was important. The psychics were always careful to add that it was Peggie's choice whether or not to have a child. It is true that a child would save our family line from dying out. Peggie was indeed the last of the Mohicans. I always had an eye on building family traditions. I passed along stories of our childhood and thrilled the children by reciting poems by Robert Service, especially "The Cremation of Sam McGee," like my father before me. I had recited it so many times Peggie also knew it by heart. We built lasting memories with special family vacations even into adulthood. I purchased high-quality items like Persian rugs, expensive china, real silverware, and diamond rings, with the idea that they would become family heirlooms. I inherited a coin collection from my father and added to it over the years. I took thousands of photographs. I preserved genealogical records, old letters, and other mementos to pass on to the next generation. I had saved my father's sword from the Masonic Temple, and my grandfather's golden watch that he received when he retired as a mechanical engineer to pass on to a grandchild. If there was no child, there would be no next generation. Our family line would die out. Even that was not the reason having a grandchild was important. The reason was simple. Only life could overcome death. Not only would a grandchild make us feel alive again, we could also rest in peace knowing Peggie would not be left alone when we died. I prayed that she would have a child, a son or a daughter, to love and to love her. Having a child would be proof to me that she trusted in the goodness of life again.

Anticipation enlivened everything we did now. We started attending to our health. We got a family dog again, a magnificent, intelligent German shepherd my husband aptly named Rex. Bred from a line of guard dogs, Rex grew to 130 pounds and had a regal, "I'm in charge," demeanor. Mike and Rex walked together every day in all the many parks around our home, and my husband began to heal. We threw ourselves into building strong connections with Peggie's husband's family, who lived nearby. We joined them for celebrations during the holidays. They attended my annual Labor Day picnic. I sat in the bleachers at middle school football games and derby car races to cheer the stepchildren. Peggie's mother-in-law and I started making plans to go antiquing together. But time dragged on, and there was no announcement of a pregnancy. I asked once about it, and Peggie said she was afraid she could not handle a baby. I assured her I would be there to help in every way, but I began to sense that there were deeper problems. She seemed strained. She didn't smile anymore. I suggested if they were having fertility problems, if the vasectomy reversal wasn't successful, they might consider adoption. There were many children who needed loving homes. She finally confessed rather bitterly that she did not want to bring a child into an unhappy, unhealthy environment. Not knowing any details behind her statement, I suggested that a child might make the situation better. Even after that idea was rejected I clung to hope, but I felt the dream slipping away like sand through my fingers.

I had a strange dream during this time. In my dream, I was looking at a series of clear glass jars lined up on shelves. The jars were like lab beakers. They were filled with a clear liquid, like water, and had lids that formed a golden band around the top edge. I lifted up each jar to examine it and noticed things were floating around in the water. I kept searching for a jar where the water was clear and pure, but could not find one—every jar was contaminated. I woke up feeling hopeless. I felt Mikey was trying to tell me something.

Peggie started running away from home whenever there was an argument with her husband. She told me her mother-in-law tried to persuade her to stick it out and face the problem head on, but that wasn't Peggie. She tended to run when there was conflict. The more she ran away, the worse the situation became. I ended up calling the police on her husband one night because I feared he was going to harm her. She called me on the phone and said he had driven them home wildly and erratically, because he was furious about something. He was speeding and careening up and down the berm along the highway. She was terrified they would crash and be killed. When they got home, she ran up into the bedroom and locked the door. It flashed through my mind that she told me he had stored a hatchet in his bedroom dresser. At the time I thought that was peculiar, but now it seemed ominous. As she talked to me on the phone I could hear him rattling the locked door. It sounded like he was trying to release the latch so he could get in. Peggie herself seemed so strange on the phone. When I told her to call the police, she didn't answer me. I wondered if she was frozen with fear. I couldn't really tell what was going on, and I was becoming frightened. All I could think was that most women are killed by their husbands or boyfriends in the bedroom. I had done my master's thesis on domestic violence, and I feared the situation was escalating out of control. In horror, I imagined him breaking into the room in a rage and axing her to pieces with that convenient hatchet. I hung up the phone, called 911, and sent the police there. We had already lost our son in a tragedy; I couldn't take the chance that we would lose our daughter in a domestic homicide. She was all we had left. I jumped into the car and raced to her house.

When I arrived, there were two police officers standing in the kitchen talking to Peggie's husband. Fortunately, the children were not home. They were with their biological mother that weekend. Peggie was standing in the hallway strangely silent, staring at the floor. She wasn't defending herself in any way. She wasn't telling her side of the story. She wasn't screaming for protection. It seemed like she was in a stupor. Her husband was barely controlling his seething rage. He seemed stunned that the police were actually there in his house. He was protesting that nothing was happening and trying to act as if he were the sane, logical person in the situation. He grabbed a bottle of prescription pills and whispered to the officers that she was addicted to pain killers. I didn't believe him, but the police seemed to consider it when Peggie said nothing. Maybe she didn't hear what he said. However, I knew the domestic violence law in Illinois because of my research. Police were required to make an arrest, even when the woman does not press charges. But there had to be evidence of physical violence—a black eye, a fat lip, some blood or bruises. There were no outward signs of abuse. Although it was obvious that something peculiar was going on, the police finally concluded there was nothing they could do and withdrew. I had Peggie get her nightgown and toothbrush and took her home with me that night. I found out she had developed fibromyalgia during this time. Her marriage—life itself—was making her sick. As a result she had become over-dependent on prescription pain killers and was sleeping all the time. It was just another method of running away.

Peggie finally told me that her husband had introduced cocaine into the marriage, and had been spending hundreds of dollars of the family income on his habit. When she objected, he spent the money behind her back. The money was disappearing to the point that she had to hide some from him so he could not waste it buying drugs. She told me that after his coke binges he'd become an abusive, angry man for days. "He'd yell around at all of us, his boys and me, and was very, very mean! The longer it went on, the worse it got. He began staying out all night without explanation, leaving me to care for his kids, never calling and just sneaking in like an alley cat at all odd hours in the morning." She began pulling away from him and immersed herself into her artwork. She believed that having a baby in that situation would have been unwise and that the baby would probably not have been born healthy. "It was a big broken dream for me. He had his kids. I didn't. And I would not have any with him!" She knew she had to get away from a very unhealthy and abusive situation. She sadly realized, "Divorce was the best thing for me." After four years, the marriage that began with so much love and promise was over. Her life had been dealt another death blow.

It is hard to express the utter sadness that reached to the bottom of my soul. All of us had been raised high with hope only to be smashed to the depths of despair once again. Following Mikey's death, the wedding had been a pinnacle of happiness. I felt as though the three of us were taken up to the stratosphere, then slammed with sadistic vengeance back to the ground. Life was battering us unmercifully once again. My thoughts turned back to a time when Peggie was a little girl. She had a Barbie doll with an extensive collection of clothes that she kept in a special pink carrying case. At that time we lived in the upstairs apartment of a two-story house. A rough gang-type family lived on the first floor. One night I reported them to the police when they fired a gun into their ceiling—which was our floor! The police officer who came to investigate the complaint was a friend of theirs, and the very officer who had fired the shot into the ceiling. We didn't get along after that. We shared a common basement where we both did laundry and stored some of the kids' toys. One day their son, Butchie, at his mother's instigation, threw Peggie's Barbie and carrying case of clothes into a barrel of burning trash. Butchie also vandalized her dollhouse by breaking all the glass windows and throwing paint in all the rooms. My father had made that dollhouse for Peggie. She had played with it for hours at a time. I remember when we discovered the destroyed dollhouse and the charred remains of the doll. There was no hope of salvaging the loss. That memory seemed to be replaying itself. Dreams of a happy family life with a grandchild had been destroyed in the same way—by a mean, selfish, grown-up child. I never understood why he couldn't just have loved her.

My daughter seemed to be in a state of disbelief that she was actually a divorced woman. She felt ashamed and angry at the same time. She had waited so long to marry. Now she felt that it was too late to try again. I was lost in my own misery. I needed to release the pain in my heart so I could let my hopes and dreams go and try to move on. With resignation I said to Peggie that I was sad to know I would never have a grandchild. To my surprise she became very angry and said she didn't need to hear that! She hissed, "It's my life!" I recoiled in shock from her harsh attitude and felt myself shrink to insignificance. She could have just listened and said she was sorry that it turned out that way. After all, she was the one who gave us hope by promising that we would be grandparents. I eventually realized her reaction came out of her own bitter disappointment, but I never mentioned the subject again.

One day I had lunch with my dear girlfriend from work who had a five-year-old daughter. She was the same friend I would talk to every morning before the work day began. She was the friend who said to me when I told her Mikey died, "I'm so sorry. I know how much you loved him." I have never forgotten those perfect words. I gave her my treasure of children's books I had collected to read to my grandchild. Knowing full well what my gesture meant, she quietly and sadly accepted them. Another dream had died.

CHAPTER 31

Adopted Grandson

I found my thoughts drifting back to the past once again, back to the good old days when Mikey was alive. It was an optimistic time when I firmly believed in the goodness and fairness of life. Of course, things were not idyllic then, but they were vibrant and engaging. In the bustling energy of everyday life there were plans to be made, goals to accomplish, and dreams to fulfill. There was involvement with family and friends as we sped toward our individual destinies. As joyous as Peggie's wedding was, it was overwritten with bitter disappointment. I needed to put everything associated with it out of my mind. What can one do with an unfulfilled dream except obsess about what might have been? I found that dreams do not die easily with me. Like water gravitating down through the filtering earth, my thoughts found their way back to another time when I thought I might have had a grandchild.

Mikey had dated a girl off and on for many years during his high school and college years. Linda was a tall, slender girl, with straight dark brown hair that hung to her waist. She was part American Indian and could have been a fashion model. She was the same age as Mikey, and was already divorced with a young son who was in the custody of the paternal grandparents. People pegged Linda as disreputable because she was flirtatious and wild. She hung around bars, smoked cigarettes, and drank too much. She was from the "wrong side of the tracks." Once, when Mikey left her house, he was beaten up by a bunch of punks who then bashed in his windshield and headlights of his new Z-28 Camaro. The reason for the attack was because he was a college kid from "snooty" Munster, the comparatively rich part of town. I don't even know where he met Linda; I suspect he picked her up in some bar he frequented. I only saw her a few times during those years. It didn't seem like a lasting relationship.

When Mikey moved to Angola to start his new career, Linda apparently visited him often. In time there was an explosive breakup. As the story goes, she "stole" his car and dumped it at a bar hundreds of miles away after they fought about his working all the time. It was a huge hassle retrieving it, and that ended the relationship. About a year later Linda called Mikey to inform him that she had a baby and he was the father. He was stunned. He didn't believe her because she had been seeing someone else after they broke up. He believed she had named him the father because he had a good job. He also thought she named the baby Michael James after him only to make her claim more convincing. It was about a year since his DUI accident; he had given up alcohol and his wild ways. He and his future wife were living together. Linda started calling them at all hours stating that she needed money to support *his* baby. Cristal was seething with jealousy. "Tell that barfly to quit calling you!" she told Mikey.

Linda retorted, "Tell that hunchback I have your kid!" Mikey didn't know what he was supposed to do. When Linda filed a paternity suit against Mikey for child support, we advised him to require a blood test to prove paternity. If the child was his, he would have financial obligations. However, I made sure he knew we did not expect him to marry someone he did not love.

While the legal wheels were turning, my husband and I decided we needed to see this little child. Linda was living with her mother in the attic of an older home that had been converted to an apartment. We carefully made our way up the rickety wooden stairway on the outside of the house and found ourselves on a narrow, unstable landing at the top. I still remember the dainty white batiste café curtains that hung over the door's half window. When Linda opened the door and we entered the small kitchen, we could hear that familiar baby cry in the background. He was in a crib tucked under the low, slanted ceiling. When I picked him up, he immediately stopped crying and looked at me with such curiosity. Young as he was, he knew I wasn't his momma! We spread his clean baby blanket out on the living room floor and laid him down there. He had only a diaper on and looked well-cared for. He was a darling little boy with a fair complexion and carrot-red hair, but I knew as soon as I saw him that Mikey was not the father. For one thing, Mikey had very big hands; this baby's hands were slender. His skin was too pink. His hair too red. However, my husband seemed enchanted with the baby, and thought Mikey might be the father.

After many months, the results of the paternity test came back. Mikey called me to let me know he was not the father. He was happy and relieved. Cristal was delighted. My lukewarm reaction surprised me, though. I mustered the comment, "Well, it would not have been a good way to have a grandchild." There was an inexplicable sadness in my heart. It wasn't only because I had become attached to the little child. I think my soul knew even then that I would never have a grandchild from Mikey. Linda faded away from our lives after that.

I remember a moment in all my despair at Mikey's funeral when Linda crossed my mind. I wondered if she had been informed. She had been out of the picture for a long time, and I had not kept track of her. I also remember thinking Cristal would be too upset if she were there because of the animosity between them. Yet, she had been a friend and should have been given the opportunity to pay her last respects. In any case, it was already too late.

Linda had to be psychic to call me out of the blue a couple weeks after the funeral. She was in a train station in Chicago on her way to visit one of her foster parents who had moved to Texas. She said she had been thinking about Mikey. She wanted to tell him she was going to Texas, because he had always talked about his adventures there. When I told her Mikey had died she screamed and cried. She just kept saying "I love him, I love him," over and over again.

After that, Linda would often call me to see how I was doing. I appreciated that someone would talk about him. She would tell me her memories of Mikey. He taught her to make tuna fish salad and how to play the war game, Risk. I enjoyed her lively conversation and loved to hear how her child was doing. She sent me a Mother's Day card the first Mother's Day after Mikey died. Cristal did not. As all the friends who knew Mikey drifted away to resume their own lives, Linda stayed in contact with me. It made me feel like the days that Mikey was alive were not over.

I also realized that I clung on to Linda and her son as a replacement for the daughter-in-law and grandchild I had hoped to have. When Mikey died, the dreams of a family life that included his children also died. At first, it was my way of coping with that added loss. I know it was an illusion, but I didn't see that it harmed anyone. I felt it was good for us all. I was able to help a child, without a father, living in less than ideal circumstances. During the years Michael James was growing up, they would visit me and we'd go shopping for his birthday. He would bring me up-to-date on all the latest computer gadgets. Linda would often call to brighten my day. She made me happy. She never forgot me.

Michael turned out to be a fine young man, respectful and humble. He joined the Marines right out of high school—even as the Iraq war was raging. He proudly told me he got a ribbon for enlisting in time of war. I admit I was relieved when he was sent to Japan to do computer work. I am proud of his accomplishments in spite of an uncertain family life. I know he wonders who his biological father is, but I don't know. I know my son was not his father, although it would have been nice had that been true. He still visits me. Now, he is the one bringing gifts—like a dainty wind chime and Godiva chocolates. He affectionately calls me Grandma Jane.

It is strange how events play out in life. Things that could be seen as an annoyance or an embarrassment can turn out to be a blessing. In the most gentle of ways, Linda and Michael pulled me back to the simple concerns of everyday life. They showed me one can find a way to survive under difficult circumstances by reaching out to others. They showed me there is more than one definition of family. As George Anderson expressed in our last psychic reading when the spirits came flooding into the room: They do give me the feeling of family, family by love or by choice.

CHAPTER 32

Existential Crisis

The years following our daughter's divorce were full of resignation. Up to that time I had been racing through a maze, searching every path possible to find meaning and happiness after Mikey's death, only to fall into a pit at the end of a wrong turn. I began to identify with those doomed lobsters you see trapped in glass water tanks in the grocery store. Even with their claws bound they still attempt to crawl up the slippery sides to escape to the freedom they see outside. The truth is, there is no way out for them, and I was beginning to feel the same way. All my life I was a person who lived planning for the future. I made plans and set goals for years at a time. It served me well in the past, but there didn't seem to be any point to it now. While I was frantically searching for answers, my grieving husband tended his garden and walked the dog. As I had not yet retired he prepared nourishing meals each day for my return home from work. When we were first married I used to wonder why he never planned far ahead like I did, and suddenly I knew. He was ten years old when his mother died, and he said he waited and waited for her to return. Finally, when he realized she was not coming back, he stopped waiting. Looking into a future without her was too painful, so he didn't look. I understood that now. He already knew the hopelessness of my quest, but he quietly let me do what I needed to do. After seven years I had depleted my energy and my optimism. I no longer looked into the future. We both now hunkered down in a place where time stood still.

We may have lived out our days in that place of "quiet desperation" if we had not been pulled out by our daughter's own emotional upheaval after her divorce. We were still parents; we still had a living daughter who needed our help as she tried to rebuild her life. We welcomed her back home to live with us until she could get her footing again. Peggie initially made a valiant attempt to find a new direction for her life. At the time Mikey died she had her own apartment and a good-paying professional job at a large corporation where she received excellent performance evaluations. After Mikey's death, she found the work environment had no patience with her grief. A coworker noticed she had a faint smell of alcohol on her breath after returning from lunch each day. It was reported to her supervisor, who also couldn't understand why her performance had suddenly fallen off. He required Peggie to go for an evaluation to find out what her problem was. "I was a psychology major. I knew I was being psychoanalyzed," she said. "They were searching for some deep-seated reason in my past for my sudden depression and my drinking at lunch. It was simple, really. My brother died! They thought there must be more to it than just that!" I doubted that they would have made the same assumption about bereaved parents. Peggie called me afterward and said, "My boss wants a copy of my psychological evaluation. He says the company paid for it, so he has a right to it."

I said, "Absolutely not. That is private and personal and you need not share it with anyone." Since her report could not be released without her consent, he did not get a copy. I felt he was just being nosy, but after that, he held a grudge against her. He tried to force her to take an unpaid leave and go for counseling for alcohol abuse. She never had been a drinker, but had turned to alcohol to smother her thoughts of suicide. Her boss was skeptical and began making the situation at work unbearable. It was apparent that no one understood how the grief of a sibling could be so devastating. Obviously, she could not return there after her divorce.

Peggie had a bachelor's degree in organizational psychology, an MBA, and solid work experience in the human resources departments at two large corporations. Yet she got few responses to the hundreds of resumes she sent out. She went on a multitude of interviews, but nothing materialized. Our country was on a binge of outsourcing jobs, resulting in fierce competition for fewer jobs. She found she could not break down that wall, no matter how hard she tried. "I felt like an utter failure in a culture that equates self-worth with work and income. The blows from repeated rejections were knocking me down further than I ever thought I could go. I finally had to lower my job expectations."

She decided to explore her artistic talent as a way to support herself. The newest home decorating fashion at the time was faux painting, so she decided to take advantage of that craze. Our home became a masterpiece as she practiced her skills. In our sunroom she painted beautiful wisteria vines against a mottled yellow background. In the living room she dabbed a dark green glaze over Palladian blue, which gave the room the feel of a pine forest. In the dining room she sponge-painted the walls to look like old plaster then stenciled grape vines around the arched doorways, giving the room the feel of an Italian restaurant. In the master bath she simulated the ripple of sunlight across water. Her work was exceptional. She secured employment with a painting crew that worked in expensive homes in the area and learned new techniques. However, the work was physically demanding with low pay, and she couldn't work at a fast enough pace to suit her employers. On her own, she couldn't find enough work. She turned to crafts and made intricate bracelets and necklaces. Her father made darling display cases for her wares. She hooked into a few craft shows, but made barely enough money to cover the high cost of booth space. People wanted exquisite handmade items at garage-sale prices.

She finally gave up artwork as a means to support herself and took a job at a nearby grocery store and pharmacy. She received high praise at first and even received an award for outstanding customer service. For some reason the situation deteriorated, and she moved on to other employment. Because she was beautiful and presented herself professionally, she got sales jobs easily in department stores and was often hired on the spot. Initially some seasonal jobs turned out positively, but the more permanent positions never seemed to last. Through our connections she continued to be offered promising positions. She got a management job in a bakery for which she was eminently qualified, because of her experience in our own bakery. She also had her MBA. I was perplexed when her far less-qualified coworkers picked on her and drove her out. She got a billing job in a doctor's office, but that ended when she was brutally berated for something any manager would regard as acceptable. She asked a coworker to fill in for her on a two-hour shift because I needed help the day I had foot surgery. She was next offered an office job in a construction business but found that boss's behavior bizarre and unprofessional. She was slowly building a career in a jewelry department of a large store and was rated a consistent top performer when she was falsely accused of ringing up other people's sales as her own. Although later vindicated, the huge corporation wouldn't reverse its error, and she couldn't afford the legal battle to get her job back. She seemed trapped in a downward spiral of repeated failures which fed her self-doubt and pessimism about life. Her work record became spotty and hard to explain to any future employers. Having blown all her opportunities, she withdrew further and further from the world and spent an inordinate amount of time sleeping.

It was heartbreaking to see her struggle so hard to no avail. I knew she took great pride in working, but I felt powerless to help her. I didn't understand what was wrong. She was obviously overqualified for these positions. Could that have caused resentment—both in others and within herself? Or do humans act like barnyard chickens that slowly peck to death any chick that becomes injured? Peggie was very emotionally vulnerable. She didn't seem to have that old fight in her anymore, and the "chickens" sensed it.

Peggie continued to date, but I was dismayed at the men she chose. At times I thought she was scraping the bottom of the barrel. She "dated down," deliberately choosing men below her in looks, education, and class. In fact, one of her boyfriends said he had hit the jackpot! Then, in a bar in a small rural town, she came across someone she gushed over as a "real catch." My jaw dropped when she told me that. This guy was a paranoid person with extreme right wing ideas about starting a revolution to overthrow the government that he was convinced was threatening to take away his guns and liberty. Peggie didn't balk when he claimed that paramilitary units were training out in the woods and the revolution was eminent. I noticed her eyes glaze over as she mentally checked out when he talked such craziness. At the same time he was a "wannabe" preacher who often quoted the Bible. Guns and religion, indeed! To his credit, he had his own modest business, and he did work, at least enough to get by.

At first he was very attentive, calling frequently, bringing flowers and gifts. It was apparent he couldn't believe his good fortune at finding such a beautiful and classy girlfriend. Then, the same losing pattern began to emerge. As the calling stopped, she began to drive hundreds of miles in all kinds of inclement weather to be with him. My husband was appalled. He was an old-fashioned European and believed the man should pursue and court the woman. I complained that this boyfriend was not protective of her safety. We began feeling we were being used as a pit stop when she would stay with him for weeks then come home for a while. It was becoming apparent she didn't feel she belonged anywhere.

Even though she was unemployed, her boyfriend began insisting that she start kicking in her share of expenses at his apartment. When he told her that the reason she couldn't find a job was that she had a college degree, she began to regret being educated. After using up all her savings, she ran up huge a credit card debt to buy groceries, of which she ate very little. In fact, because she often starved herself, her teeth began to rot. Still, she clung to him, ignoring all the warning signs that this was a desperate and detrimental relationship. She claimed she loved him, but I didn't believe her. Like the battered women I had interviewed for my master's research, I believed she used the excuse of love for not taking responsibility for herself. For seven long years, she was willing to sleep on an air mattress on the floor of his shabby apartment strewn with broken dishes and dirty underwear. She was willing to endure a sad relationship to maintain the illusion that someone was taking care of her when she could not take care of herself.

My sister Sarah always loved Peggie and saw in her a gentle soul. Sarah believed she was punishing herself for being alive after Mikey had died. Did she feel guilty for being the only surviving sibling? Someone once told me she thought her father believed the wrong child died. I was shocked she could possibly think such a horrible thing. It was absolutely untrue and hurt him deeply. Both my husband and I wished we could have died in Mikey's place, but it never entered our minds to wish our other child had died instead. My husband was a blunt person, and he tended to be overcritical. He'd frequently criticize her self-destructive behavior and continued to do so as she struggled to rebuild her life. It would take a person with high self-confidence and self-esteem to withstand his painful honesty. Being very sensitive and unsure of herself, she probably interpreted this as his not loving her. I reminded her that he had been equally critical of Mikey's alcoholism and berated him mercilessly until he straightened up. As an immigrant who had to pull himself up by the bootstraps, he expected his children to put forth their best effort to succeed. Actually, he was still fighting for her to turn her life around. He had not given up on her. He often had tears in his eyes when he spoke of the way she was throwing her life away. She couldn't seem to recognize the love beneath his gruff manner. At the same time, I didn't believe harsh criticism was the way to turn her around. I tried to tell him that she was an adult and would make her own choices, and we could only continue to be there for her. Neither approach was working.

When I recognized how distorted her thinking had become, I sadly wondered if she harbored similarly negative thoughts about me. I wondered if she viewed our devastating grief over Mikey's death as evidence that she wasn't "enough." Did she feel I cared more about having a grandchild than I cared about her? How could she not see I would always love her, with or without a grandchild? Over time I saw so many people reach out to her in friendship, but she just didn't notice. As her extended family clustered around her, she often appeared oblivious to the kindness they offered. She used every excuse to avoid family gatherings, because she felt that she was being judged as a failure. It became apparent that our daughter's divorce was more than a breakup of a marriage. Piled on top of her brother's death, it became an existential crisis that brought forth deep issues of unworthiness that that had plagued her all her life. The crushing weight of so much unhappiness and disappointment had laid bare her soul.

As if there had not been enough misery, our German shepherd, Rex, died suddenly of stomach bloat. I came to find out that it is a condition that affects large, deep-chested dogs and kills instantly. We came home to find him dead after going to a movie on Valentine's Day. He was only six-and-one-half years old, half his expected lifespan. We had never cried so hard at the death of a pet, but this animal was unusual. We have had many dogs, but Rex felt like a human being, like a person. Other people said the same thing of him. Rex had given us comfort and helped us heal. I bitterly concluded that everything we dared to love would be taken from us.

Recently, Peggie offered me her perspective of those tortured years after her brother died. "When I lowered my expectations about what kind of job I could get, that thinking must have spilled over into every part of my life: my relationships, my dress, the way I ate. I didn't care about myself anymore. Only in lowering my expectations did I find anything I could regard as positive. That is the course my life took when Mikey died—*lowered expectations*. I came to the conclusion that nothing I knew I deserved in life was ever going to be. We had to take what we were given and not expect any better. Even though I had made a promise to Mikey to live life to the fullest—to carry on in his honor, basically—it seemed that was impossible. I had learned at every turn that life would never get back to what it was supposed to be. I began to feel tortured by life. What would happen next to show me how miserable life is? When would it ever change? I learned to be grateful for what I did have, even though it was not what I really wanted. After all, I was still alive. Everything was taken from Mikey. Everything! How dare I expect more?"

CHAPTER 33

The Turning Point

At first it sounded like just another job. One of Peggie's cousins had frequently urged her to apply for employment at a grocery store where she herself had worked for many years. Since Peggie had been unemployed for another long stretch, she accepted a minimum-wage job there. At the most unexpected place and at the most unexpected time, she found herself precisely where she needed to be to meet the person who would be the turning point in her life. In meeting him she realized that the yearning inside her had never truly died. Her high expectations for her life were still there, hidden deep in her heart. She described her first reaction when they met, "At first I thought he was too good for me. I quickly took stock of myself and didn't recognize who I had become. I could not believe that I had such low self-regard that I thought I did not deserve someone as wonderful as he was. I guess I had given up on what I deserved or expected out of life when Mikey died. Thankfully, I recognized Prince Charming when I found him, in spite of all the years of tortured, cloudy thinking."

Her eyes sparkled whenever she saw her "shining light." Everyone started commenting that Peggie appeared radiantly happy. I saw her smile again. In fact, she seemed to giggle at absolutely everything.

He was a wonderful young man who adored her and treated her well. I found him to be intelligent, ambitious, energetic, responsible, handsome, and *normal.* He had a positive outlook on life that was refreshing. She says they complement each other—he the responsible oldest sibling, and she the more flighty youngest. He is talkative and outgoing; she is quiet and reserved. They built a successful home-based online business together. "We are a great team. We are so good together that we are making our dreams come true."

Without realizing it, we had given up doing many pleasurable things after Mikey died. Peggie quit listening to music. I stopped playing the piano. I couldn't bear to put up a Christmas tree. Of course, her boyfriend didn't know any of this. When he told Peggie he was coming to our house come to put up a Christmas tree, Peggie wasn't sure if we would allow it. But, how could I have refused such a kind and innocent offer? After fourteen years we had a Christmas tree once again. We put the tree in the sunroom where all the windows made a showcase for it. I resurrected what was left of our old ornaments and carefully added each one as I used to do so long ago. The tree came with hundreds of tiny colored lights that twinkled warmly through the snowy woods, welcoming us home. On Christmas Day the four of us celebrated with a delicious dinner of steak au poivre, baked potato, Brussels sprouts in a white sauce, and our famous cranberry amaretto Bundt cake. I dug out my Christmas piano music, and we sang carols together. In the evenings when I was alone I would sit near the tree and feel at peace. It was a symbol of the rebirth of hope and joy in our lives.

Peggie and her boyfriend recently moved into the little house on our property that we call the cottage, or the cabin. Peggie always thought it would be "awesome" to live close to us. I must admit it is wonderful to have her so nearby. Few parents are as lucky. In our society children tend to move far away, following their careers. We always had a very close mother-daughter relationship. Peggie had always refused to move too far away from us. Through all our years of unrelenting grief, we stayed close to each other. All we really had was each other, and that still is true. Sometimes she and her boyfriend stop in for lunch when Mike makes some extra food. Occasionally I bake them a batch of chocolate-chip cookies or a dish of stuffed green peppers. Peggie keeps her art supplies in my art room and comes over to paint. Together we painted an old dining room table with whimsy designs, letting our imaginations soar. The table turned out so cute that people would exclaim, "I want that!" or "It looks so San Francisco!" or "You could get a fortune for it on eBay!" This past summer Peggie and her dad began gardening together. He showed her how to plant vegetables and kept her water barrels full. She also grew baby's breath, carnations, and forget-me-nots along her patio. Her living so close is a comfort and a blessing.

Peggie and her boyfriend have been together several years now and seem very happy together. It appears these years of a loving relationship have shown our daughter what she needed to know—that she still deserves the best, that happiness is still possible. Having someone love you and treat you well is a healing experience. It brings out the best in one's character and builds a psychological bulwark against life's storms. Yet, I sometimes feel a twinge of apprehension. I realize that my optimism about life was shattered when Mikey died. Without consciously realizing it, I expect to be blindsided by some unforeseen event at any moment. I also have learned that whatever happens, we will survive. We have already survived the worst and have still found joy in life. So, I do not worry anymore if something will last forever. I just try to appreciate what is before us each day.

Recently, Peggie had another turning point. She needed a haircut, but as her usual stylist was on medical leave, she had to accept a substitute. She believed this sequence of events truly was not a mistake. The substitute's name was Raymond. When he asked about her siblings, Peggie told him about her brother's tragic death. His response was remarkable.

Peggie said, "He immediately expressed sympathy and wanted to know the details. When I began to tear up, he ran and got tissues for me. He saw my pain, even after sixteen years. He did not ignore it like most people do. He was truly disturbed by the news, which was remarkable for a complete stranger. His empathy created the vital connection that caused me to open up to him, and he to me. It opened up my wound; he saw it and took it head-on. The most important message was that he absolutely, without a doubt, believes we are all reunited in the afterlife. His conviction was solid. I asked him how he knew.

"His response was, 'faith.' It was the usual response I got from everyone else. The difference is that he took it a step further and asked me, 'Why not believe? What good is there from not having that hope and belief that you will see your brother again?' Why wallow in misery, not believing? Why be tortured by negativity when it only brings more misery? It was so refreshingly logical. I told him I used to have signs, after-death communications, that gave me hope. I told him about the blessing bird dream I had shortly after Mikey died. I told him that Mikey had taken my hand in the dream like he always had done in life and showed me a wonderful, glowing bird. I felt as if I had been with my brother in that dream, and I have never forgotten it.

"Raymond asked, 'Why not cling to those truly astonishing moments of the only proof you have? Why not just let go and believe?' I felt a huge weight lift off my shoulders and my soul.

"He went on to ask what I would have wanted for Mikey if I had been the one to die instead. Of course, I agreed I would want him to live a long, happy life—even more so because I couldn't. I would want Mikey to keep and live out the exact promise I made to him when he was killed. Raymond drove home the point that my continued misery actually shows that I don't think Mikey would want me to live a full, happy, healthy life. It would show I think less of him, and I absolutely don't! Raymond told me that from this day forward, every time I think of Mikey, I must smile and not cry. Remember all the years of good and not his tragic death.

"I came home from my hair appointment that day glowing with a new positive outlook on life. I have decided I will smile when I think of Mikey! That's a hard one, but I'm going to give it my best shot!"

CHAPTER 34

Writing the Story

The Indiana Dunes National Lakeshore is a unique park at the southern end of Lake Michigan. It is a place I have been familiar with all my life. As a child, I remember swimming there in the summer and hunting for coins in the sand in the winter. My husband and I enjoyed many days there on the beach with our own children. Of course, we spent many hours boating on the lake itself. When I retired we bought a beautiful piece of acreage in the dunes area. It had a little cabin, a large pond, and enough room to build another house deep in the woods. We named our property Still Waters and hoped it would restore our souls.

In winter, the southern end of Lake Michigan is often subject to lake-effect snow. When the icy north wind blows across the lake, it acts like a giant snow machine, generating white-out conditions in communities along the shore. One never knows where the capricious column of snow will set up, but the blizzard passes as quickly as it arrives, leaving the area blanketed with deep drifts of pristine snow glistening in the sunlight. I love to walk through the woods on our property in the winter after such a storm. The air is crisp and invigorating. Sounds are muffled. The rays of sunlight streaming through the tall, spindly trees create intricate patterns on the snow. The rattle of the dried oak leaves still clinging to the ice-coated branches catches my attention; I smile at their stubborn endurance. I enjoy these winter walks the most when spring is just around the corner. The air is milder and the days are beginning to lengthen. I look for signs of rebirth, marveling at the resilience of life. Before the last snows are melted, the purple crocus peeks through the dead remnants of last season. As the sun approaches the vernal equinox, my husband starts listening for the distinctive gobble of the migrating sand cranes. He excitedly calls me outside when he spots them circling so high in the sky we can barely see them. They are catching a current to ride back north again—obeying the ancient pattern of their species. When the barren trees sprout their first tiny green leaves, the frogs begin their song in the shallow pools of water in the wetlands. As the frog serenade increases in intensity, I feel a peripheral apprehension building in my own psyche. First the forsythia blooms, then the lilac, and then the rose. When I glimpse the first lightning bug in the dune grass on the slope down to our pond, I realize that June is upon us. In the past these were comforting signs of continuity. Now, as the earth tilts to awaken new life, I am forever reminded that the day is approaching, the summer day when Mikey died.

I no longer consciously dwell on the circumstances of Mikey's accident. I don't torment myself any longer about that moment when he realized his fatal error. It was a freak accident on the one hand. On the other hand it was as if he were answering a clarion call to fulfill his fate. Yet, the fifteenth anniversary of Mikey's death hit me with a resurgence of grief I did not expect. There are some who say it is just another day, but the body knows otherwise. June 15th is seared into my memory as if with a branding iron, and this anniversary coincided with Father's Day. In my despair I wrote an e-mail to my sister-in-law Dolores who I always found to be an intelligent and perceptive listener.

> Dear Dolores,
>
> Today is Father's Day. It falls on June 15th this year, and this June 15th marks fifteen years since Mikey died. It is a day of conflicted emotions arising from a symbolic conjunction of events witnessed only by us from our bereft perspective.

> Father's Day is a symbol of the joyful day Mikey was born. June 15th is the tragic day he died. The passage of fifteen years has not healed the wound. It surprises me that each anniversary of his death is not any easier. It's true the pain isn't as searing as in those first years; yet, it is just as painful—maybe more so—because the world has moved on and I have not. I cannot.
>
> The truth is, I still cannot accept that he died. It makes no sense to me. He had so much to offer the world. He was interesting and interested. He was honest and laughed easily. The world needed him. We needed him. I think often of the story you told of when he would ride his bicycle all those miles to your house in the country just to visit. You said he was such a nice, unassuming young man. Our kids grew up together, so you knew him. You remembered how he taught himself his arithmetic before he went to kindergarten. From the time he first announced to me that some numbers are all-together and some numbers are not-all-together, he delighted me with his unique perspective. What I miss most about him is that he always had something new to tell me, something he had just learned, something I didn't know. Now, even in his death he is teaching me something I didn't know. I didn't know that grief would never end. He was a remarkable person, and I miss him.
>
> Love,
>
> Jane

It is hard to deal with the realization that Mikey's death strengthened our marriage. It is a blessing that I don't want to accept or even recognize, because the price was too high. I didn't ask for it and I didn't want it, but there it was anyway. A sacrifice that made petty grievances fade away, and led us to love each other again. We had learned in The Compassionate Friends that the death of a child will either tear a marriage apart or make it stronger. Yet, even before learning that divorce statistic, my husband and I instinctively clung to each other. We were the only ones who truly understood what we had lost. We were the only ones who knew the whole story of Mikey's life; how he came to be; how much we loved him; how much he meant to us. We were unmarried teenagers deeply in love. With our love, we created him. With our love, we raised him. With our love, we buried him. With our love, we remember him. It is the love of him that brought us together and keeps us together still.

As I've finally lifted my gaze to look back over all the years since Mikey died, I became aware that there were those who never gave up trying to help us heal. The most devoted of those was my sister, Sarah, who always remembers Mikey's birthday on June 23rd. She chose to remember the day he was born instead of the day he died. On his birthday, flowers would usually be delivered to our door with the note, "In celebration of Mikey's life." One June 23rd she came to our house with a car full of helium balloons. We wrote love messages to Mikey on them with felt-tip markers and then released them into the sky and watched them until we could see them no more. Two different years she sent us live Painted Lady butterflies in their tiny, cooled containers to be released on his birthday. This past year she sent two-dozen exquisite roses in rainbow colors. I thank her for never forgetting. She tells me she will never forget. In her gentle way, she has been turning us away from dwelling on his death to celebrating his life.

Sarah has a fascinating freelance occupation as a show production manager, which affords her travel to many locations in the world. She also loves to travel for pleasure both in the United States and in Europe. Wherever she travels she always visits a local church to light a candle for Mikey. There she says a prayer to ease our pain, and asks Mikey to stay close to us so we can feel his presence. She began doing this the year he died when she took a sabbatical in San Francisco, California. She continues her devotions to this day. She lit a candle in Sedona, Arizona, at a beautiful church built into the red rock of the canyons. She lit a candle in a church high up on Holy Hill in Wisconsin. She has been to Paris five times in the past ten years and has lit candles in churches all over that city—twice in the gothic Notre Dame Cathedral seeped in thousands of years of history. She also lit candles in countless small churches in southern France's Loire Valley: Avignon, Saint-Rémy-de-Provence, Arles, Aix-en-Provence, Tours, Les Baux, and in Gordes, high on a hilltop. She's lit candles in Nice, France, in Wiesbaden, Germany, and in many churches in Rome, Italy, most notably the gold-encrusted St. Peter's Basilica in Vatican City. She lit a candle at the church where Princess

Grace and Prince Rainier III were entombed close to the castle on the highest hill in Monte Carlo. She's lit candles in Florence, Italy, in the Tuscany region—the cradle of the Renaissance. Her work will next take her to Barcelona, Spain, where she says she will keep the flame of love burning for our dear Mikey.

My husband began lighting a seven-day vigil candle in our home soon after Mikey died. We buy special religious candles in beautiful colors: rose, gold, green, purple, light blue, dark blue, red, and pure white. There is always one burning on our fireplace mantle, even these many years later. A burning candle evokes a spiritual connection. It is like keeping a light on for someone who is away from home. It says, "We have not forgotten you. We are waiting until we are together again." We have never attempted to forget Mikey, thinking we would be happier. Instead, we speak of him, because he is in our hearts every moment. We set a place for him at Thanksgiving and Christmas tables; Peggie signs Mother's Day, Father's Day, and birthday cards with both her name and her brother's name. As comforting as these rituals may be, they are still laden with sadness.

There came a time when I knew I needed to find joy in my life again or die of a broken heart. My long, serious illness earlier in my life had taught me an important lesson: the way to get well is simply to be happy. So, I consciously began a "program" to get happy. Although I had balked at first at getting another dog, my husband took me to see a German shepherd puppy that stole my heart. We named him Rommel, but Romeo would probably have been a more fitting name because of his sweet nature. I changed my TV viewing habits. In the past I had always preferred to watch serious news programs and documentaries. I now forced myself to watch the comedians on late-night talk shows, hoping to be persuaded to laugh. And I did begin to laugh. I began tutoring math, because I like the optimistic energy of young people, and because math reminds me of Mikey. I started a tradition of annual picnics on Labor Day so all the family can gather together. Having lots of people around me has always buoyed my spirits. We occasionally went to German dances or to a good movie. We've built two new houses, creating beautiful havens in the hope that the beauty of nature would nudge us to healing. I participated in Native American sweat lodges seeking spiritual meaning in ancient ceremonies. It was easy to find happiness in the past before Mikey died; now it felt like such hard work. It would be like trying to paint after going blind. You know the motions required; you know the correct brush to hold, and remember which color to use. In spite of the determined effort, the outcome just doesn't make the grade. Underneath it all, I was still crying. I could not seem to stop crying.

For years, I had the nagging feeling that what I needed to do was write this story. I had made attempts to begin writing several times but found it difficult to focus. I had always loved writing. I was a very quiet child and found that I needed to write to express myself. When I was older I found that writing was a way to sort out my thoughts or to pull up feelings from the subconscious by giving them form in words. Through writing I'd hoped to find answers or meaning in Mikey's untimely death—or a modicum of peace.

Sometime after the fifteenth anniversary of Mikey's death, my writer's block dissipated like fog in the sunshine. The words began to pour out of me. It was like being awakened from a long, silent winter of grief. As I relived those days when Mikey was alive I felt as if the clock had turned back to those happier times. I felt energetic and enthusiastic, often staying up after midnight absorbed in my task. I looked up the music he loved. With the aid of the wondrous Internet, I was now able to listen to the same concerts on YouTube that he had attended many years ago. As I reread his letters and postcards, his journals—including the journal of his AA program—and his school notebooks, I began to see his life from a wider perspective than that of a grieving mother. I began to see him as a vibrant and interesting individual who lived his life with zest and curiosity. I began to appreciate him as a person independent of our family relationship. I could now see an individual on his own journey through this life.

As I remembered his life, a tremendous peace washed over me. I was overwhelmed with gratitude that he was born and that he loved his life. Even knowing the excruciating pain in store at losing him, I would still have wanted to be his mother. He was the perfect son for me and for us. No family could have loved him more. Who other than a math major could have understood his obsession with numbers at four years old? Who but an avid skier could have taught him how to ski? What little sister could have been more devoted? As

I listened to the tapes of the psychic readings, I finally took to heart the beautiful message that his life continues and that we will meet again one day. My sister Carole said we cannot fully understand what happens at death until we face it ourselves. Until then, it will remain a beautiful mystery. Miraculously, as June 15th loomed this year, I found that the dread of the approaching day was no longer there. The excruciating pain had softened. It was *almost* like any other day. I had learned that grief never ends. The more important lesson, the lesson that shown forth in everything we had done all the years of his life and all the years since his death, is that love never ends. It is in that knowledge that I have found peace.

CHAPTER 35

Ridin' the Storm Out

Michael is my sister Carole's son and Mikey's cousin. He had come for his sister Caroline's graduation party on our sailboat dock those many years ago, which was the last time the family had seen Mikey alive. Although we thought we were gathering to celebrate Caroline's graduation, I wonder if we were truly gathering to bid Mikey farewell. For both celebrants, it was a new beginning. Since Michael left to drive home to Arizona right after the party, we were not able to contact him while on the road. So he was not present at Mikey's funeral. After he arrived home and learned the news that Mikey had been killed, he wrote a wonderful eight-page, handwritten letter to us. It is the most beautiful letter I have ever received. I have included a portion of it as the final chapter. It has taken me sixteen years to fully appreciate and thank him for it.

> Dear Michael,
>
> Today is June 15th, and it is sixteen years since Mikey died. Every June 15th we do something special to honor Mikey's memory. I decided that today I will write a thank you note to you for the wonderful letter you wrote to us right after he died. At the beginning of the year I started to write a book

about all the things that occurred around the time of his death and in the years that followed. I hoped that through writing his story I could make sense of his tragic and untimely death and, perhaps, find a measure of peace. In preparation for writing I needed to go back through the all the papers I saved, e.g. the letters he wrote, the letters we wrote to him, the engineering report about his accident, and the tapes of the psychic readings. I also went through all the letters and sympathy cards I received after he died, finding comfort again in each one. I came across the magnificent eight-page handwritten letter you had written to us. Both Mike and I re-read your letter, and after all these years it still had the power to deeply touch our hearts. Frankly, it brought tears to our eyes once again, tears of gratitude for your thoughtfulness and memories of Mikey. They were unique memories that only you could have written.

So, today, I want to thank you for this beautiful prayer you offered from your heart in our time of greatest need. You said you didn't know if we would find it "comforting or disturbing, blasphemous or holy," but you tried your utmost to soothe our aching souls. Although your letter certainly did soothe us at the time, I think our pain was too raw and our thoughts too tormented to be able to calmly enjoy the beauty of your words. I actually think we appreciated your letter even more reading it sixteen years later. So many years have passed and everyone has gone on with their individual lives—as they should. We often feel left behind by life, stuck in a place where time stands still. Finding your letter has brought us comfort once again.

I must have asked you about spiritual places to visit, because you eloquently described five places in and near the Colorado Plateau. One was the Organ Pipe Cactus National Monument in Arizona near the Mexican border. It was your letter that inspired us to take the trip there that first Christmas after Mikey died. We met you and your new wife Jenny in Ajo. I was so pleased to see you were wearing one of Mikey's T-shirts I had sent you. We all hiked the park together. I had found an old detailed map among Mikey's papers on which he had marked his path through the park. So, we were able to follow in his footsteps. It was the best possible way for us to spend

> that first Christmas. I have never forgotten it. You ended your letter, "Come to Organ Pipe this Christmas and together we can pray and beseech the stars for an answer." As I write this story I am coming to the conclusion that in the end, that is all we can do.
>
> We love you dearly.
>
> Aunt Jane and Uncle Mike

I will always remember that long trip to Organ Pipe that first desperate December. We drove cross-country over seemingly endless roads for hour after hour, too numb with grief to feel our fatigue. The movement of the car seemed to soothe our souls, and having a destination gave us a purpose in what had become to us an irrational world. My thoughts are still haunted by the many crosses along Route 86 outside of Tucson, Arizona, where people evidently had been killed in accidents. We stopped and looked at a few of the memorials. Some were elaborately decorated with artificial flowers, beads, mementoes, and handwritten notes. I had never seen such a desolate stretch of road with so many markers of tragedy. Yet I found a strange comfort in them and wanted to linger there. It made me think of my mother, who always wanted to visit any little overgrown cemetery she saw along the roadway. We would patiently accommodate her, but never understood her need. I understood now that it was a place to find common ground with sorrow.

We stayed at a beautiful old bed and breakfast in Ajo that stood in sharp contrast to the surrounding landscape devastated by strip mining in years past. The house had been the mine manager's home. It reminded me of the old, sturdy homes of the wealthy in the Southeast. On Christmas Day we were served a delicious prime rib dinner in a dining room with high windows curtained with old lace. We were the only guests. The place was for sale. When I asked the proprietor about the many memorials alongside the road coming into town, I was told that the Indians who lived on the San Xavier Reservation were often drunk and wandered down the unlit highway at night and were hit by cars and killed. The depth of historical sadness in that nonchalant statement made me shudder. I identified with those bereaved souls who lovingly tended those tragic memorials. We were to do the same in the years to come.

The trip to Organ Pipe was the first of many trips we took in the years after Mikey died. Driving in a car is meditative, and we continued to seek out places of solitude. We stayed off-season at the Big Powderhorn ski resort in northern Michigan where Mike and Mikey had skied together. My husband pointed out a certain chalet where they enjoyed a hot tub after a cold day of skiing. He recounted another time when Mikey ate five huge steaks at an all-you-can-eat steak dinner during a ski trip in Traverse City. Peggie joined us when we drove to Door County in Wisconsin without reservations one Labor Day weekend. We learned never to do that again, when we could not find a room within a hundred-mile radius. We sojourned many times in Bayfield, Wisconsin, where we sailed around the Apostle Islands in Lake Superior and enjoyed incredible gourmet meals at Maggie's Restaurant. On our ferry boat cruise around the islands we were informed that the water of Lake Superior is the purest of all the Great Lakes because it is the deepest. The beaches were clean, beautiful, and mostly unpopulated. Our dogs loved romping in the shallow waters. One year, Peggie and I stayed at secluded McQue cabin on Madeline Island. It was late August and the nights were so cold that we sat in the sauna just to get our bones warm. My husband and I always took time to drive the long, winding road through the Chequamegon National Forest. We would drive for hours and never meet another car. The smooth motion of the car combined with the sunlight flickering through the tall trees was hypnotic, inducing a reverie of years long past.

Recently, my sister Clarissa and I took a nostalgic trip back to Erie, Pennsylvania. It was a mini-reunion with some cousins on my mother's side whom we had not seen in over forty years. We were meeting a few of the relatives for the first time. As children, we'd spent summers at our Aunt Chris' summer home high up on an eighty-foot cliff overlooking Lake Erie. My mother parent's were poor Hungarian immigrants who raised nine children in a house next to the shipping docks. After the last of my mother's siblings had died, the family secret was finally revealed in a book written by David Frew entitled, *Midnight Herring*. Her four brothers had been rum runners on Lake Erie during Prohibition. The Eighteenth Amendment had made it illegal to buy alcohol in the United States. At the same time, it was legal to buy alcohol in Canada, but illegal to drink it there.

It was hard not to take advantage of that absurd situation! We met with the author of the book, who had written several books about the shipping history of Lake Erie. He had interviewed our Uncle Joe with the understanding that nothing would be published until after his death. Uncle Joe, who was "incredibly bright," was the mastermind of the rum-running operation. He was very good at fixing boat engines and leveraged his talent into getting a piece of the existing operation on the lake. Finally, he designed his own boat called the Gray Ghost that had a steel hull, sat low in the water, and could outrun the Coast Guard. With his brothers he set up his own rum-running operation between Erie, Pennsylvania, and Port Dover, Canada. When the Chicago mob started to move in on the action, he and his brothers retired. Prohibition was repealed shortly after that. How Mikey would have loved to learn that bit of juicy family history! I had so many questions, but all the older generation had died, including my mother. There was no one to ask, "Why didn't you tell us?"

On the way driving home from Erie our route took us right past Angola, Indiana. It had been at least a decade since I had vowed never to return there. I decided I could not pass by the roadside where Mikey had died without stopping and paying my respects at that hallowed ground. I was relieved to find that the cross had been returned to its original position and the lovers' initials on the stop sign were gone. Nothing else had changed. The corn was planted once again. The little house where the old woman lived who called for help that day had not changed. The little barn up Buck Lake Road was still there. The traffic still tore past at a high rate of speed in both directions at the T-intersection where Mikey met his fate. I laid a dozen red roses there at the foot of his cross and wished things could have been different.

CHAPTER 36

The Letter

August 19, 1993

Dear Aunt Jane and Uncle Mike and Peggie and Cristal,

Some years ago in December (of 1985, I believe), Mikey came to Arizona, alone. One place he sojourned was Organ Pipe. He explored it on foot, scaling the lofty Mount Ajo on the eastern border of the park. From that vantage point through the clear winter air he had a vast tramontane view, range after range of craggy desert peaks, each silhouetted behind the previous in ever fainter shades of purple, each etched in stark contrast along its ridge and fading below into hazy valleys of creosote. He looked east, north, west, and south far into Mexico; surrounded by desert, his eyes beheld little of the works of man. And how far could he see? Those hard-edged mountains seemed close enough to touch … twenty … fifty … one hundred miles? The eyes see, the mind cannot fully accept or understand. Indeed, how far can any of us see?

He then came north to Flagstaff, and together we set out on a winter hike in that mightiest of gorges, the Grand Canyon. Being December, the days were very short and a ranger tried to discourage us. Through a small lie and considerable persistence we got her to grant us a permit for a two-day hike that normally required three days or more. What the hell!

Down the New Hance Trail we plodded, one of the most rugged on the South Rim, into the bowels of the earth. The trail was built by one man in the latter part of the last century to mine asbestos at the bottom of the canyon. The mine proved unprofitable, and ever-resourceful John Hance (or "Captain" Hance as he fancied himself) became the first tourist guide at the Grand Canyon. A prolific storyteller, he delighted in regaling children with tall tales of how he'd dug the canyon himself. One day, an insightful young girl asked matter-of-factly, "But, where did you put all the dirt?"

He had no answer and even on his deathbed wondered aloud, "So, where do you suppose I could've put all that dirt?"

Ever downward we went, from ponderosa pine forests of knee-deep snow at the rim, through stands of pinion and juniper, and into a desert not unlike that at Organ Pipe. At the bottom, in this wilderness of dry rock, raged the mighty Colorado River, beaten to a white fury in the rocks of Hance Rapid. A long, cold night, a tent saturated with dew, an early start the next morning, and a long, ever-upward trudge. How far up? Imagine four Sears Towers, one stacked atop the other. If you stood in the viewing room of the topmost one, you could still not quite see out over the rim of the canyon.

So, we kept moving, upward and out, knowing daylight was in short supply. One step forward means one less to go. Fatiguing, yes, but the beauty of the place! Up through ancient rocks of the Hakatai Shale, so deep and red it seems to stain the retina. There in the rock are petrified sand ripples a billion years old, locked into stone when jellyfish were the most advanced form of life on earth. The walls of the canyon tower above, so tall they seem to lean over us, and behind them we have occasional glimpses of the rim itself, dusted in snow, impossibly remote. Upward through the strata, which lay like pages of a book, a book of earth history covering a time span three hundred and fifty thousand times as long as all of written human history. It tends to put things in perspective.

Upward, ever upward. Here is where I see the essence of Mikey, the unflagging spirit and boundless energy. A shining wit, a touch of vulgarity, quick to laughter—so full of LIFE! I think of him now, on that dusty trail, plowing forward, unfettered by the high altitude. Hot blood courses through his veins, his lungs take in great gulps of air, muscles contract and relax as he thrusts his body forward and upward. A powerful man, powerful in mind, body, and spirit. Indomitable. It seems an unforgivably cruel twist of fate that such a vibrant soul could be snatched away. Why? Where is the meaning in this? Is it in the silent brooding rocks of these canyon walls?

We come to a side canyon in this barren marge of stone, and there stands a majestic old cottonwood. It is winter and so the tree has no leaves. But, it is a familiar tree to me, an old favorite, and I have slept beneath its boughs many times, seen its rich green leaves vivid against a background of red rock. I have heard its leaves whisper in the breeze ... was it trying to convey secrets I am too crass to comprehend? Now, it stands starkly, silently, naked branches thrust harshly into a hard blue sky. It is a façade of death, for we know it lives. Is this an analogy to the apparent finality of death? This cottonwood "dies" every fall, is "reborn" every spring, and has been repeating this cycle for decades. And so it is all around us. Life and death are profoundly intertwined like the deep roots of this cottonwood, and one is not possible without the other. Tiny life and death dramas play themselves out all around us constantly. The shrike impales a mouse on the thorns of a mesquite tree. The mesquite silently battles the parasitic mistletoe. The giant saguaro stands stoically over it all in mute eloquence, all the while its seeds consumed relentlessly by harvester ants.

We talk of the web of life, but a web is static. Life flows like a river, but a river flows in one dimension. Life is like a flowing web, a shimmering, restless maelstrom that defies understanding and makes no distinction between life and death. It is all part of a vast, incomprehensible flux, turning in on itself in a continuous dance of destruction and creation.

When I look at those bright stars suspended over the cactus of Organ Pipe, I think of the atoms that constitute my body, how they were forged in the core of a massive star in its final hours, were then spewed into the void in its dying spasms, and ultimately incorporated into the living tissue of my body. This I see in the death of a star the seeding of life. So be it with Mikey. He is gone, but lives on in our hearts. He will be there at Organ Pipe this Christmas, and every Christmas hereafter. And I have every intention of hiking the Grand Canyon with him over and over again, forever.

Love,

Michael and Jenny

Mikey on the edge of the Grand Canyon

Epilogue

My favorite picture of Mikey is one his sister took of him lying on the edge of the Grand Canyon in Arizona. We had taken a family vacation following his graduation from high school, driving our Buick station wagon from Indiana across the wide, western expanses to see this most magnificent of the Seven Wonders of the Natural World. In those days one was able to walk up to the very edge of the canyon in several places along the rim. Peggie snapped a picture of Mikey in his cut-off blue jeans and black cowboy hat lying flat on a stone ledge overhanging the canyon. He was gazing across the canyon at the breathtaking grandeur before him, totally unafraid. Although my heart skipped a beat when I first saw the picture, I knew it captured his essence perfectly. After he died I had the photograph enlarged and framed. I hung it over my couch in the family room to always remind me that he loved to live on the edge. He was a daring spirit and unafraid of life. Some might see this as a fatal flaw that led to his tragic death. But, is this really a flaw? Isn't that the way to live life? Isn't how you live more important than how long you live? You don't judge a beautiful painting by its size, nor should you judge a beautiful life by the number of years. When I look at that picture, I am humbled by his courageous choice to embrace life without fear.

In writing Mikey's story, I was reminded that we are all individuals, each on his own journey here on earth. However one wishes to understand it, we come into this life with certain talents to use or certain lessons to be learned. It is important to respect and understand that only one's soul really knows what its path should be. I believe now that part of my journey was to write the story of a tragic death, unending grief, and eternal love. In writing this story I also hoped to end the silence and loneliness surrounding grief and mourning in our culture. People grieve far longer than most are willing to acknowledge—often forever.

A Sister's Promise

Mikey and Peggie as children

My promise to my dear brother, Mike

Growing up with you was a joy and a privilege. You were my friend, my companion, my idol. We were inseparable. You were the one I could always look up to. I was always so proud and eager to proclaim, "That's my brother!" You gave me more than a million reasons to seize every possible chance to brag about you to everyone.

You were the one I could always count on when I needed anything, to be there when I needed you most. You were always ready to lend a hand. And you knew how to do everything! You were brilliant! You even saved me from drowning when we were small. You were always an excellent swimmer! You were always there to protect your little sister.

I always wanted to be just like you. I remember your calling me "copycat" when I would imitate the things you would do—like eating the same cereal that you did for breakfast, your favorite: Frosted Flakes.

You have given me so many fond memories.

Like the time we gazed out our bedroom window one Christmas Eve and actually heard Santa's sleigh bells!

The times we would walk to the pond and catch tadpoles and bring them home to watch them grow into frogs.

The times we actually fit in the compartment behind the backseat of the Volkswagen Beetle.

The times we would snuggle up and listen to the rainstorms, counting the seconds between the lightning and the thunder.

The time we took a canoe adventure up to Canada. You were always the adventurous one. The river was too low, so you got out and pulled the canoe—with me in it.

All the times we rode the Ferris wheel at Kiddy Land. When we got older we would ride the "Zipper," with you rocking the car so hard that we would flip upside down. And we were laughing the whole time!

All the ice cream cones we ate at Dairy Queen—especially when we would whisper "Dairy Queen" in the backseat just loud enough for Mom and Dad to get the hint and pull in.

All the times we roller-skated in the basement of our town house.

All the nights we lay in our bunk beds talking until we fell asleep. All the tents we made with our sheets. All the car rides in the country giggling hysterically in the back seat. All the trees we climbed. All the hills we rolled down. All the fields we ran through—with Spike right by our sides. All the lightning bugs we caught. All the fish you caught, cleaned, and fried for us. All the happy times at Purdue. All the football games. All the rock concerts. All the days at the beach playing Frisbee until we got so hot that we would race each other to the lake. All the music albums, even eight-track tapes, we listened to together. Especially the time we were totally oblivious to the fact that your steak and hash brown dinner was burning to a crisp downstairs, setting off the smoke alarm! We had to open all the doors and windows, in the dead of winter, to air out the house before "the parents" got home. All the trails we hiked together in Minnesota. All the sunsets and stars we gazed at together. All the snowmen and igloos we built in the winter. All the times we raked all the leaves in a pile and leaped in and rolled around. All the times we walked to the corner store to buy candy, you holding my hand all the way. All the laughter and happiness we shared!

I will miss you forever!

You were always a free spirit, doing what was dearest to your heart. You gave me inspiration to live life to the fullest, for this is how you lived. In everything you did, you gave it your utmost all and did it with your full heart and soul. Your fervor for life is reflected in the beautifully perfect things you created and surrounded yourself with. Your beautiful wife, your lovely home, your perfectly "engineered" garden, the love and joy you gave to all of us are reflections of who you stood to be. And you stood tall and proud—as we do for you.

Your spirit will never die as it will be forever held deep within our hearts. My promise to you, Mikey, is to never let go of the love and joy you gave me, to keep you and the beautiful memories you gave me close in my heart forever, to remember your laughter, your smile, your beautiful laughing eyes, your strength, and your courage.

I promise to be your eyes.

To see and behold all the beauty in the world.

To see the birds nesting, eating seeds, and bathing.

To see the rainbows and the shooting stars.

For you.

I promise to be your ears.

To listen to the songs of the birds in the sunshine and lullabies of the crickets and frogs in the moonlight.

To hear the flapping of the wings of doves.

To hear the laughter of the loons at dusk and the howl of the wolves at the moon.

For you.

I promise to be your senses.
To smell all the beautiful flowers, the scent of a spring shower, a Freshly cut lawn, and a campfire with roasted marshmallows.
To taste all the perfect vegetables you have grown and all your favorite foods.
To feel the sun's rays warming our hearts.
To feel a summer rain cooling our faces.
To feel the sand between our toes and the waves rushing under our feet.
For you.
I promise to experience, learn, and love everything I possibly can for you as only you would do it—with all my heart and soul.
I love you forever, my dear brother, Mike! You shall never be forgotten. Never!

Love forever and ever,

Peggie

Peggie and Mikey as teenagers making a graduation toast

About the Author

Jane Quint lives in the Indiana Dunes area with her husband Mike and their German shepherd, Rommel; her daughter Peggie lives close by. She holds a Bachelor of Science in mathematics from Purdue University, a Master of Science in computer science from the Illinois Institute of Technology, and a Master of Arts degree in sociology from the University of Illinois at Chicago. She is retired from a career as a software engineer in the telecommunications industry. Her husband owned and operated Quint's Bakery in East Chicago, Indiana. *A Cross by the Road* is her first book.

Bibliography

Blank, Jeanne. *The Death of an Adult Child.* Series Editor, John D. Morgan. Amityville, New York: Baywood Publishing Company, Inc., 1998. Copyright © 1998 by the Baywood Publishing Company, Inc., Amityville, New York. All rights reserved. Printed in the United States of America on acid-free recycled paper.

Bohm, David. *Wholeness and the Implicate Order.* New York: Routledge, Chapman and Hall Inc., 1992.

Bowman, Carol. *Children's Past Lives.* New York: Bantam Books, 1998.

Bowman, Carol. *Return from Heaven.* New York: HarperTorch, 2001.

Cayce, Edgar. *Circulation File: The Akashic Record: Edgar Cayce Readings.* Virginia Beach, VA: Edgar Cayce Foundation, 1971.

Cooper, Paulette and Paul Noble. *The 100 Top Psychics.* New York: Pocket Books, 1996.

Frew, David. *Midnight Herring: Prohibition and Rum Running on Lake Erie.* Erie, Pennsylvania: Dispatch Printing, 2006.

Gibran, Kahlil. *The Prophet.* New York: Alfred A Knopf, 1955.

Kaku, Michio. *Hyperspace.* New York: Doubleday, 1994.

Kubler-Ross, Elisabeth. *On Death and Dying.* New York: MacMillan Publishing Company, 1969.

Langley, Noel. *Edgar Cayce on Reincarnation.* New York: Warner Books, 1967.

Martin, Joel and Patricia Romanowski. *We Don't Die: George Anderson's Conversations with the Other Side.* New York: Berkley Books, 1989.

Millay, Edna St. Vincent. *And You As Well Must Die, Beloved Dust,* Lines 9 – 14.

Mogenson, Greg. *Greeting the Angels.* Series Editor, John D. Morgan. New York: Baywood Publishing Company, 1992.Copyright © 1992 by the Baywood Publishing Company, Inc., Amityville, New York. All rights reserved. Printed in the United States of America.

Moody, Raymond. *Life After Life.* New York: Bantam Books, 1975.

Moody, Raymond. *The Light Beyond.* New York: Bantam Books, 1989.

Moody, Raymond. *Reunions: Visionary Encounters with Departed Loved Ones.* New York: Villard Books, 1993.

Strommen, Merton, and Irene Strommen. *Five Cries of Grief.* San Francisco: HarperSanFrancisco, A Division of HarperColllins Publishers, 1993.

Von Franz, Marie Louise. *Psyche & Matter.* Boston & London: Shambhala, 1992.

Endnotes

1. Mogenson, *Greeting the Angels*, xi.
2. Ibid., xiii.
3. Blank, *The Death of an Adult Child*, 197.
4. Ibid., 224.
5. Ibid., 224.
6. Ibid., 60.
7. Bohm, *Wholeness and the Implicate Order*, 15.
8. Ibid., 149.
9. Von Franz, *Psyche & Matter*, 40.
10. Ibid., 204.
11. Ibid., 206.
12. Ibid., 207.
13. Ibid., 236.
14. Langley, *Edgar Cayce on Reincarnation, 169.*
15. Moody, *The Light Beyond*, 7.
16. Cooper, *The 100 Top Psychics*, 69.
17. Gibran, 32.